A Brief History of White Nonsense:
The Throughlines of White Privilege that Keep Racism Alive

Craig Pelkey-Landes

Copyright © 2023 Craig Pelkey-Landes
All rights reserved.
ISBN: 979-8-9885469-2-4

DEDICATION

To my wife, Fortana, and daughters, Elena and Corina.
You are the reason I hope and strive for a better future.

ACKNOWLEDGMENTS

Thanks especially to two readers of a very early draft, Trina Roach and Jim Henderson. Your excellent suggestions helped me create a stronger narrative.

Thanks so much to Sarah Augustine for writing the forward. Your framing of this book as a counter to the gaslighting so prevalent in the discourse about US history is spot-on.

Thanks also to D. Scott for editorial insights that helped clarify points and improve the book immensely.

Thanks to Ken Gingerich for the amazing cover design.

Finally, thanks so much to family and friends who believed in me and the importance of this topic. You all helped me push on past imposter syndrome and fatigue to get this book to the finish line.

CONTENTS

Forward..1

Introduction..5

Chapter 1: Finding the Throughlines of White Nonsense............14

Chapter 2: Throughline: Inventing Race, Presuming Superiority....20

Chapter 3: Throughline: Maintaining the Social Hierarchy
       of White Nonsense...44

Chapter 4: Throughlines: Progress and Regression...................76

Chapter 5: The Hard Work of Dismantling Systems..................95

Resources...104

Forward

Reflections on Gaslighting
By Sarah Augustine

The last time I saw my mother alive, we had the same exhausting conversation we had had many times before. She explained – again – why the details of my childhood – the chaos, violence, and my ultimate abandonment by her – were either:

1. Not that bad "you survived, didn't you;" or
2. Caused by external forces of chaos beyond anyone's control "that was considered normal then;" or
3. My fault, because my childhood-self chose to live with my violent, mentally ill father rather than with her (I hadn't).

From visit to visit over the better part of two decades, she trotted out various characters whom she felt should share blame. My father, of course, was the central perpetrator in our well-rehearsed trope, abetted by: a patriarchal church (true); various teachers and social workers that could see the signs but didn't care enough to intervene (true-ish); my sister, who demanded my mother forget about me (complete bullshit); and on and on, always someone else. Never herself.

The history agreed to by all concerned is that when I was in the 8th grade, she purchased a lime-green station-wagon and drove across the country to pursue a bright, unencumbered future. I was left to grow up with a violent schizophrenic and without contact from her.

I didn't blame her – she was a co-victim, and she stayed alive by saving herself. What troubled me throughout our relationship was her denial of what happened to me.

These conversations were devastating for me because her denial of my past attempted to invalidate all the choices that came after. My identity as an activist and advocate for others like me - those whose lives are shaped by structural violence - was born from lived experience. The denial of my lived experience calls into question my response to it.

I loved my mother desperately – she was a life-preserver in the black, turbulent sea of my childhood, which was a horizonless world without direction or relief. She had been the one provider of affection and gentleness, my safe harbor. And she left me in a dark, dangerous place, to grow up without her. In her absence, I was intermittently homeless, or lived in a two-bedroom apartment that often housed ten people, where strangers, some of them dangerous and none of them stable, moved in and out while my father moved in and out of incarceration.

Years of hunger and abuse caused damage, of course, yet according to her, the damage I sustained was my own fault somehow. She initiated this conversation every time I saw her. She rationalized what happened, challenging my life story and my understanding of reality. The popular term for this type of psychological abuse is gaslighting.

I refused to agree with her version of my life. My sister told me many times, if I would only go along with her story, our mother would stop the nonsense of blaming the world – blaming me – for what happened. She needed all her children to agree on a fiction she invented – that the world is safe, and nothing too bad happened in our shared history. My unwillingness to go along with the party line was painful for our mother, my sister told me, and if I would only get on message, our relationship would improve, and family gatherings would improve for everyone. But I could not.

I did not refuse to accept her version of history to defend my pride, but because I longed to be known. How could I have a meaningful relationship with my mother if its foundation – our shared origin – was based on fiction? I haven't thought about this part of my life for a long time. But reading Craig Landes' book brought the experience of gaslighting to mind.

The way our country talks about race and the history that has brought us to this moment sounds very much like the denial that was practiced diligently in my family, where abuse was normalized. In this work, Craig Pelkey-Landes posits that we cannot have a meaningful relationship as a country while we consent to a shared narrative that is based on fiction. "White nonsense," which he defines as the fiction of held tightly in our shared national narrative, results in structural inequalities that justify the inherent supremacy of some over others.

Pelkey-Landes argues that if the generalized "we" in the United States could clearly understand our history, we would quit asking why racism still exists. We would not be shocked by the election of a president whose platform was based on a desire to reconstruct the blatant White privilege of the 'good old days.'

He points out a posture of erasure in our collective narrative that denies our shared colonial past by ignoring it. This mutual consent to willful ignorance obscures the streaks of ugliness that shoot through the dominant culture, right down to laws and policies that uphold racial supremacy. Those who refuse to participate in the comfortable narrative of erasure are marginalized, like activists in the Blacks Lives Matter movement and the movement to resist extraction on Indigenous lands. They are told to stop complaining and to get with the program if they want things to improve. Their stories scrutinized and invalidated, these activists must grapple with both inequity and gaslighting.

A Brief History of White Nonsense

Our national history is replete with examples of domination by the powerful followed by justifications for why taking more than one's share is morally just. Pelkey-Landes provides an unflinching account here with forthrightness, humor, and aching clarity, with the intention of making the truth "as accessible as possible" to everyone.

He tells us the cycle of white violence and the resistance to that violence will not come to an end until we acknowledge past wrongs wrought by white-supremacy, and then intentionally work to dismantle systems of inequality in our country's institutions.

Craig asks his own people – White Americans – to come to the table and reckon with a past that has brought us to this moment, where inequality still reigns despite some visible examples of wealthy or powerful folks of color. He is clear in his charge: if we want the cycle of violence to stop, our systems must change.

He says no to the convenient story that everything is fine – resisting the denial that makes White folks feel comfortable. He is the faithful relative staging an intervention in solidarity– asking loved ones to tell the truth – so that the entire family system can finally heal.

I am thankful to Craig for stepping forward in the human family that makes up this country we both call home. It takes courage to object to a narrative that makes our friends and relatives feel comfortable. Craig chooses to stand with the oppressed by calling on White folks to begin at the beginning – to tell the truth, which is the first step on the road to repair.

Sarah Augustine is the Executive Director of the Coalition to Dismantle the Doctrine of Discovery, a national coalition with global reach. A Pueblo (Tewa) person, Sarah has represented the interests of Indigenous community partners to their own governments, the United Nations, the Organization of American States Inter-American Commission on Human Rights, The World Council of Churches, and a host of other international actors including corporate interests.

Introduction: Why Am I Writing This?

There is a particular set of challenges in US American society that just doesn't go away. Sometimes we reach a boiling point, a time when those who have been marginalized by the roots and branches of racism say "enough!" and a critical mass of white people also take notice that something is very wrong. These are also times when some in the (bare) majority white culture push back and say, "There's nothing to see here. No racism happening now, and let's not dwell on the past or even examine it very closely. Move along!"

I write during one of these times. Why does it seem like we are all on edge about race these days? As I write this, the nation has been experiencing a reckoning with a specific kind of violence against Black bodies after the nine-plus minutes a white police officer spent strangling George Floyd (almost casually, with a knee) while several other officers stood and watched, and while shocked and horrified bystanders recorded it, wondering what the hell had just happened. This is just one of countless instances of such violence.

As I write this, the nation has experienced an attempted coup. In response to anxiety about their place in society, white nationalists descended on Washington, DC and attempted to overturn the results of the 2020 presidential election by force when they stormed the Capitol building on January 6, 2021.

A Brief History of White Nonsense

Why is this happening? Why does this cycle of white violence and resistance to that violence keep happening in every era of US history?

I'm writing to try and answer these questions. I'm writing because I believe we face these challenges again and again because we don't understand our history and haven't really come to terms with it. A shift in demographics away from a clear white majority is catching up with the increasingly tenuous status quo. What's this status quo? I'm calling it White Nonsense.

White Nonsense, at its core, is the fiction of race. It is the fiction that people originally from Europe whose skin lacks melanin are inherently of more value than people with varying degrees of melanin. White Nonsense is the invention of the fiction of white superiority that paved the way for white privilege. White Nonsense describes how white privilege has undergirded and undermined our history and our experiment in constitutional democracy. Because of White Nonsense, the world we have created is off-kilter. The lie of white supremacy keeps morphing and adapting, so the fullness of constitutional democracy has never been fully realized.

Why is some random white dude writing a book about racism in the US? I'm writing this book because I hear some version of the question "Why does racism still exist in America?" or even "Does racism really still exist in America?" all the time. This book is a brief attempt to answer that question.

The germ of the idea for this book started at a school board meeting. School boards have been a hotbed of a certain brand of conservative activism in recent years. The school district where my kids were educated is a prime example of this. After running on a "lower taxes" platform a slate of candidates for the Pennridge School Board quickly showed what they were really there to do.

It started with a controversy over how textbooks were vetted and brought into the curriculum. There was a middle school geography textbook that members of the school board had a problem with. They presented the problem as one of processes. This was a process that had been developed by trained educators and had been used effectively for years prior. Privately, there were two problems: first, a section where they didn't think Donald Trump was getting fair representation. In a book about geography written shortly after he was elected. What?? Second, they did not like the definition of "socialism" the textbook gave. The curriculum committee pointed out that this was, in fact, the correct definition of the word. The board members did not budge, and the textbook was removed.

The issues cascaded from there. After the Marjorie Stone Douglas school shooting there was an action on campus—a group of students walked outside to protest during a school assembly they felt did not address the root of the issue well enough. Over 200 kids took part, and some parents joined them. My youngest was there, and so was I. The kids got weekend detention, which caused a bit of a stir—but I had no problem with that. Nonviolent direct action can have consequences. Plus this kind of punishment often serves to amplify the issue, not squash it.

Next there was an off-campus event about school violence. A school board member showed up in an NRA t-shirt. I guess neither the 1st nor the 2nd Amendment protect you from being an asshole.

As I write this, the board has moved on to fake outrage over the teaching of the unambiguous facts of history, couched in opposition to "Critical Race Theory." Pennridge, of course, is not alone. They are part of a wave of white fears about changing demographics and how to talk about the skeletons in our collective closet. Their actions around the curriculum got me wondering why white people are so afraid to examine US history—especially the roots and branches of white supremacy. The unambiguous facts of history are easy to find and the throughlines are easy to trace. Facing and understanding that history is another story.

A Brief History of White Nonsense

But this is not a book that scapegoats white conservatives. White liberals are the beneficiaries and the propagators of White Nonsense, just like their conservative counterparts. I'll never forget watching an episode of Saturday Night Live in November 2016 just days after Donald Trump was elected president. One sketch in particular stood out.

The setting was an election-night watch party in NYC. The group was mostly white, with two Black people in attendance. It was supposed to be a clear win for Hillary Clinton, and the vibe of the sketch reflected that. But as the results came in, the white Hillary supporters at the party became increasingly horrified, until the impossible happened: the election was called for Donald Trump.

For me, the lesson of the sketch was that "progressive" white people had been coasting along on an arc of history that was bending toward justice, and we were basically just along for the ride. This shit was easy. We, along with some of our more centrist white counterparts, voted (twice!) for Barack (Hussein!) Obama, after all. Our progressive forebears had enacted laws against all the overt forms of racism we could think of, so things were definitely headed in the right direction. The election of a woman as president was just part of that beautiful march of progress.

But in the SNL sketch as in real life, the tide turned as election night wore on. At midnight, one of the white characters says, "Oh my God. I think America is racist!"

The election is called for Trump, and the white friends at this party-turned-wake are shocked. But not the two Black attendees. This was just another Tuesday in America, and the results were anything but surprising. The sketch ends with a white friend saying, "This is the most shameful thing America has ever done!" The two Black friends get a good laugh out of that one.

What the Hell Just Happened, and Why Does It Keep Happening?

On January 6, 2021, a mob of angry Trump supporters tried to violently enter the nation's Capital and overturn the election results of 2020. Lives were lost among both insurgents and Capitol police. This was a largely white group, motivated by grievance against the waning influence of whiteness and egged on by Donald Trump's blatant and repeated lies about election fraud and thinly-veiled calls for his followers to "take their country back."

Trumpism didn't arise out of a vacuum. Demographic changes that are bringing US citizens of white European ancestry out of a full majority of the population have been documented for years. This, as scholar Ashley Jardina points out in her book *"**White Identity Politics**,"* has led some white US Americans to become fearful that their position of power is in jeopardy. For some this is a conscious fear, and for others, it may lie somewhere in the subconscious.

The precarious position of whiteness in the US came into sharp focus with the election of Barack Obama. The election of Donald Trump is widely, and I believe correctly, seen as a reaction on the part of white US Americans to these demographic shifts.

After a single term, Donald Trump was defeated, and hopefully by the time this is published he will be facing severe legal and financial consequences. But we see clearly in the careening from the presidency of Barack Obama to Donald Trump that racism has not been solved. Not by a long shot.

Though the 2020 defeat of Trump at the ballot box is good news, Trump's support was and remains staggering. Even with his approval ratings in the low 30s, that's a lot of approval for such overt racism. And the sense of grievance among his largely white following points to the ongoing challenge of White Nonsense.

A Brief History of White Nonsense

Why am I writing this book? If we do not understand where such grievances and fears come from, we cannot possibly understand the present and work toward a world free of White Nonsense. There are a lot of excellent resources out there to delve into the problem of race in the United States, but I wanted to create a resource that could serve as a brief introduction and overview—to make understanding this history as simple and accessible as possible.

You may think that "White Nonsense" is a term that puts some white people on the defensive. I have made the conscious decision to use this term as a way of decentering and deemphasizing white comfort over and above the unambiguous facts of history. Plus, it's attention grabbing and kind of funny.

For many, as the SNL sketch so vividly demonstrates, the election of Donald Trump was inconceivable. But it is just an asterisk in a centuries-long enterprise that created and perpetuates the concept of whiteness.

Why does this stuff keep happening?!?

This is the question I keep asking myself as I delve further into White Nonsense. From a disregard for Black bodies to outright ignoring the identity and rights of Native Americans, why does this stuff keep happening? The racism that we see today does not exist in a vacuum. Its roots go deep in our society. They start before the American Revolution, and even before 1619 when a ship carrying enslaved people landed at the English colony of Virginia. The White Nonsense we're exploring here is the origin of the fiction of race and its throughlines that we are experiencing today.

This is an exploration of the origins and ongoing problem of White Nonsense, from before Columbus right through to the overt white nationalists who tried to violently overthrow the election of Joe Biden, from the perpetrators of outright violence against people of color to the Chads and Beckys of the world questioning the rights of

Black and Brown people to have a picnic, walk in a park, order a frappuccino, and just live their damn lives without being hassled.

This is an exploration of how the world has been organized for the past 500-plus years in a cloud of legal, religious, and cultural White Nonsense. The persistence of White Nonsense presents constant threats to personhood, well-being, and life itself for people of color.

Friends sometimes wonder about me. "Why is it always about race with you, Craig?" Well, because the history of the United States is all about race, all about managing that original premise—that white people are inherently better. The struggle of our common history as US Americans is to unpack the depths of that original misconception. It's all about race for me because people came here, exploited the land and the people who already lived here, and brought other human beings to be used as instruments of free labor. And yet somehow, from the time white Europeans decided to cross the Atlantic through today, white ideas and experience are the barometer of what is "normal" and "right."

The building of this country and the challenges we face today all come back to the construct of race and the damage racism is still causing us as a nation. This book is about examining the unambiguous facts of history to demonstrate that basic premise.

Coming to Terms with Our Common History

I think when we either don't understand where racism is coming from or don't know why it has not stopped, that is a lack of historical perspective. I'm not even blaming individuals for that. If you never had an opportunity to learn something, if the data wasn't there for you to process, if information was kept from you to keep you or the gatekeepers of information from feeling "uncomfortable," that's not exactly on you. But the truth is that the clear, unambiguous facts of history are out there, in plain sight. This stuff is completely knowable, so a common history *can* be established.

A Brief History of White Nonsense

In order to get that perspective, we need to go back to the beginning of White Nonsense and trace that nonsense right into the present. A look at the historical record will clearly show those throughlines. This is not revisionist history, at least not in a negative sense that some would like to use that term. Fuck that noise. This is what happened as people who came to think of themselves as "white" stumbled onto what became known as the Americas. This is what happened as people who needed to think of themselves as white kept trying to plow the consequences of their actions under a veneer of progress and change.

In the beginning of White Nonsense, white people had ships, guns, and a newfound sense of boldness in the face of an earth that was suddenly no longer flat. What would they do with all of these coalescing tricks of fate? Take what was theirs and then take what was somebody else's, that's what!

But what if they found others on this round earth? Well, those others probably didn't share the white people's belief system, and they probably didn't structure life the exact same way white people did. And white people knew that to be other than they were—in any way—was just wrong.

So in order to justify the exploration and resource extraction they had embarked upon, they needed to justify their behavior. On the face of it, they were invading territory clearly occupied by others. But they wanted to take that territory for themselves. They needed a framework to justify this rush and push to occupy already-occupied land.

A Note on Brevity

For the purposes of brevity and clarity, I am focusing on three groups of people: European Americans, African Americans, and Indigenous communities who were here long before colonization. There are many other groups I could write about and perhaps will someday. Asian Americans have a particular history in relationship to White Nonsense that needs to be explored. And Latine people are in the bizarre position of being among the first colonizers but somehow—perhaps since they have a range of complexions from light-skinned to darker-skinned—not seen as white in the same way as others of European descent.

So, while the fiction of whiteness has found many other groups to vilify, scapegoat, and harass. Europeans, African Americans, and Native Americans provide both a breadth of context and a narrow focus for a brief look at the power and, ultimately, moral poverty of white privilege.

This is a short book. It is not meant to be an exhaustive look at every moment between the mid-1400s and today, with every nook and cranny of the subject explored in detail. The more research I do, the more stories I find that clearly demonstrate the throughlines of White Nonsense. There will be a lot that is not covered here. But there are plenty of resources I will list at the end to deepen your understanding of the throughlines that brought us here.

As a little taste, I offer a preliminary glimpse at the roots of the concept of race and its implications for the present.

Chapter 1: Finding the Throughlines of White Nonsense

This book arises out of a number of questions. When it comes to the pervasiveness of racism, we all have questions.

- Why doesn't racism just disappear? We ended slavery and have laws against discrimination, so problem solved, right? Does that make it a problem of a "few bad apples" who do all the racism?
- Why can't we all just get along?
- What are Black people so upset about these days?
- What are white people so upset about these days?
- What are Indigenous people so upset about these days?
- I wasn't an enslaver / wasn't enslaved. Why should I care about this?
- Don't all lives matter?

These questions have answers, but you can't find them without understanding White Nonsense. Without understanding the roots of the concepts of race and racism, answers to these questions remain lost in a mysterious cloud of personal prejudice and personal behaviors. That ain't what we're talking about here.

A Brief History of White Nonsense

And before we go forward, here's what I mean when I use the term "racism." Racism is the witting or unwitting use and abuse of white privilege. Looking at racism is not about being anti-white. It is about understanding the roots and branches of white privilege that keep racism alive. If you are willing to deepen your understanding of these roots and branches, you will be less likely to dismiss current events around race as some unsolvable puzzle. You (I'm talking to you, white people) will be less likely to be nervous about groups that have been historically marginalized by white privilege just wanting to matter.

Our history and current events show that there is much more to racism than personal prejudice and behaviors. The concept of race and especially the idea of a racial hierarchy have not existed since the beginning of time. They have historic roots and can be traced back to a very specific, relatively recent period of time. Understand these roots and the branches that still grow from them and we will have a much better shot at answering the questions that persist here in the present.

They say that history is written by the winners. And before the Internet, I would definitely say that was true. Access to information and how "the story of us" got told was in the hands of the people in power, i.e., people who thought of themselves as "white."

These days, information is plentiful. It's a fire hose. That is good and bad. The bad is all too familiar. Information devoid of fact-checking can breed misinformation and conspiracy theories not grounded in any evidence or data—or with shaky evidence and little data. The firehosey nature of information means we are drowning in it. So even though history is now not just the domain of the "winners," there are challenges to understanding our true common history.

On the other hand, there is an upside to having access to information and a means of disseminating that information to whoever wants it. Take, for instance, someone like me—with a writing background and an interest in history, along with the nagging questions of what brought us here and why we're not much, much further along.

A Brief History of White Nonsense

I can dig for the facts and let the fullness of history—at least, what I am able to uncover—speak.

The facts, as we will see, are there for anyone to see. But the concept of whiteness demands a certain narrative. Building a common history based on unambiguous facts seems like "revisionism." Nobody wants to dredge up bad times, but they happened. It is important to celebrate positive events in history, but it is also important to understand the unpleasant and downright evil parts of our common history. Because those parts can impact the present like nine-plus minutes of a knee to the neck.

Let's get to telling the fullness of that history, so we can stop the cycle of White Nonsense and celebrate this dynamic, multicultural nation in which we have always lived.

I have little idea what kids are taught in school these days, but when I was growing up, American history started with the Pilgrims and ended with stamping out the spread of communism in Asia. Sure there were some rough patches: slavery, the Civil War, and then all a sudden, 100 years later, a civil rights movement. European settlers braved the frontier to carve a nation out of godless wilderness. Eventually the West was "won." And there was plenty I never heard anything about until I was much older and satisfying my own curiosity on the history of these United(ish) States. Tulsa Race Massacre? Never heard of it. Pueblo uprising? What's that?

I will say, I was blessed with parents who welcomed my curiosity from a young age. At Scholastic Book Fairs and the like, I purchased books on Harriet Tubman, Frederick Douglass, and George Washington Carver. I grew up in Arizona, and I remember a picture book about the daily life of a Navajo girl. That's not to say I was a "woke" kid, got the whole story about these icons of African American history, or had a clear understanding of day-to-day life in the Navajo Nation. But I wasn't raised in an "America: love it or leave it" context, for which I am grateful.

So I had some pieces of the history and some small understanding of the present. But the historic pieces of this crucial business of race were never sewn together.

The power of White Nonsense has not been extinguished, I believe, because white US Americans don't want to confront our history and undo the nonsense. Not enough of us, and not badly enough. Until this privilege is confronted and undone, we will continue as a nation to be slowly undone by the lie of white supremacy.

This book is an attempt to lay out the facts of history in support of this premise. I believe the facts of history are clear, and the answers to all the "why" questions can be traced back to the Doctrine of Discovery, the codification of melanin-based race as a concept, and a made-up racial hierarchy with whiteness at the top.

I believe that, as demographics shift, this hierarchy is finally showing signs of crumbling. But we see in current events how embedded into all our systems racial hierarchy is. White privilege is not going away without a fight.

Finding a Way Forward

In the broadest of strokes, we all want roughly the same thing. We want a good life for ourselves and our families, and to make some small impact on the world. Whatever our background, wherever we come from, we are all George Bailey—not sure, but hoping we matter in some small way. But mostly we just want to live our lives, enjoy as much of it as we can, stay positive, and make a positive impact on the world in some tiny way.

Race and racism are the ultimate in uncomfortable things to think about, especially for people who identify as white and don't really want to think about the long legacy of the lie of white supremacy.

So I get it. It's easier not to think about this stuff. You are busy just trying to live your life—why should we ponder this sad, heavy stuff?

A Brief History of White Nonsense

Because it affects us all and our ability to have a happy and fulfilled life. That may seem like hyperbole, but it is the thesis of this book. All that was stirred up as Europe in the 1400s began to look beyond itself, all the justifications required for the land- and people-grabs that followed are still reverberating into the present. White Nonsense impacts nothing short of our life, liberty, and pursuit of happiness.

Even as there is a broad movement to better understand the roots of White Nonsense, there is a countermovement that would rather you avert your eyes and plug your ears. For too many, this is a history that they would rather not examine. Political leaders fight to exclude a complete look at our history in classrooms and libraries. They say this kind of project is teaching people to "hate America." They call an examination of the unambiguous facts of history just a different kind of racism. Ha! That is obviously a huge pile of bullshit.

So just for the record: I do not hate the United States. I love the land of my birth. I love this experiment in democracy that at the moment seems to be careening toward authoritarianism in response to honest questions and a search for a deeper understanding of our common history.

I want to understand this place as fully as possible. If the founders imagined forming a more perfect union, I want to be all about working to get it right, to get it ever more perfect. If Navajo code talkers could help win WWII, if people like John Lewis and Shirley Chisolm could fight for the promises held in the founding documents, I can certainly see that potential—untapped and unfulfilled as it may be—and still love my country.

So in direct answer to critics of a full and honest exploration of our common history (if I were writing a memo, it would begin: "Dear Tucker Carlson and Candace Owens…"), here is what this book is not:

1. It is not about teaching white people to hate themselves.
2. It is not about teaching people of color to have a "victim mentality."

The historical record and current events show that there is no greater peril to the forming of a more perfect union than the roots and branches of white privilege. That is why it is so imperative we understand and put an end to White Nonsense. Recent history gives us a real sense of the fragility of democracy under the weight of white privilege.

To understand that history and heal the present, we need to go back past the civil rights movement, past the Battle of Wounded Knee, past Black Wall Street, past the Civil War, way back to when sailing across the ocean blue was not even a flicker of an idea in Christopher Columbus's mind.

The Heart of the Problem: Discovery

One particular historic set of circumstances can help explain why we are still dealing with the reverberations of racism in the 21st century. Those circumstances were the process "discovery" of what has come to be known as North and South America by European explorers and the exploitation of sections of Africa by European governments.

How did they justify taking land already occupied, and taking people themselves as property? Let's find out.

Chapter 2
Throughline: Inventing Race, Presuming Superiority

This book is, I believe, part of a wave of collective energy. It is part of a movement of people trying to bring our common history into our collective consciousness as US Americans.

What is it that too many of us have not been taught? We learn about slavery—that's no secret. We learn how Native Americans were driven off land they'd occupied. But all of that is in the past. People who identify as white collectively (mostly) feel bad about it, but what does our treatment of people back then have to do with now?

Finding the connective tissue between then and now is the task many of us are pursuing, with books like this. We understand what happened then, but I believe we haven't explored WHY it happened and keeps happening in different forms. We haven't sufficiently explored how that "why" reverberates into today. Why did slavery exist? Why were Native peoples treated as a nuisance, expendable? Why are Black and Brown bodies treated as nuisances and expandable even today?

It comes down to the invention of "whiteness" and the ongoing preservation of whiteness as a social construct that requires a position of superiority to survive. Does that sound too extreme? The throughlines we'll be exploring in this book will bear witness that this is exactly the world we live in. These are the unambiguous facts of history.

A Brief History of White Nonsense

The Land Before "Discovery" and the Concept of Race

Before the invention of whiteness, before Europeans stumbled onto the shores of what some Indigenous cultures call Turtle Island and which Europeans renamed North America, there were (and still are!) vibrant cultures thriving here.

Most of us have a vague sense that people lived here before 1492, but we don't really know what that looked like. The ability to ignore and not understand what was here before—that is a prime example of White Nonsense at work.

The most important thing to understand about the history of North America is that human beings inhabited the place going at least as far back as 16,000 BCE.

The most common hypothesis is that humans crossed from Siberia over an icy Bering Strait, went through what is now Alaska, and from there populated what is now North and South America.

An interesting side note: the most ancient human remains found in North America were, until fairly recently, thought to be those discovered off the coast of California, dating back some 13,000 years. Then a fossilized footprint was found in the White Sands National Park[1] in New Mexico. Whether they came down from the Bering Strait or had some kind of floating vessel from islands in what we now call the Pacific Ocean is still being researched.

The point is, 15th century Europeans figured out there was this land mass across the Atlantic Ocean over 30,000 years after other humans found it. There were cultures, governments, languages, etc., all doing just fine before Europeans came on through. Europeans happened to have more deadly weapons and came bearing unfamiliar

---

[1] Laff, Michael. "The oldest human fossil footprints in North America." *ShareAmerica*, 4 October 2021

and therefore more deadly diseases, which made all the difference when coming to extract commodities from an already-occupied land.

So before jumping into 1492 and thereafter, let's take a brief look at what we know about who was here well before then.

Clovis Culture

Our understanding of what was going on in the Americas before European colonization is always growing. Among the earliest people to become indigenous to Turtle Island are the people who developed what anthropologists call "Clovis Culture."[2]

Clovis refers to the town in New Mexico where a distinctive spear or arrowhead was discovered. Why is an arrowhead a big deal? Archaeologists believe Clovis tips to be among the first inventions of the original-original settlers of the new world. Clovis Culture goes back to at least 13,500 BCE and stretched as far north and east as modern-day Pennsylvania and as far south as Venezuela.

There is ongoing debate and new data emerging every day that points to cultures existing before Clovis. In any case, this distinctive tool/weapon offers a key to understanding some of the original residents of what we now call the Americas.

Woodland Culture

In what is now the eastern part of the United States, Woodland Culture emerged around 1000 BCE (Mitchell Museum of the American Indian).[3] So while the Celts were knocking around in

---

[2] Mann, Charles C. "The Clovis Point and the Discovery of America's First Culture." *Smithsonian Magazine*

[3] Mitchell Museum of the American Indian. "Mitchell Museum of the American Indian Woodlands Culture Area Map." *Mitchell Museum of the American Indian*, https://www.mitchellmuseum.org/education/documents/3WoodlandsLessonPlanFINAwithheaderL_000.pdf.

western and central Europe, Woodland Culture was taking shape, from southeastern Canada through the eastern US to the Gulf of Mexico.

Woodland culture developed leather crafting, textile manufacture, stone and bone tools, and ever-more elaborate shelters. There was a shift from a more nomadic existence to the establishment of more permanent village settlements during this time. Pottery with elaborate decoration was a feature of Woodland culture.

So, language, culture, religion, agriculture in many forms was flourishing in North America long before Europeans built boats that could cross the Atlantic Ocean and stopped being scared of what was in the ocean or some imagined edge of the earth.

Just as Europe has ancient roots in groups such as the Celts, Vandals, Iberians, and Vikings, so it is with the US. Out of Clovis. Woodland, and other ancient cultures, many Indigenous groups grew. In the Southwest, there were the Hohokam, Diné, and Pueblo communities, among many others. Shoshone, Wichita, and Osage, in the Plains; Creeks, Cherokee, and Apalachee in the Southeast; Algonquian, Iroquois, and Delaware in the Northeast. So many cultures and so much ancient history were already here when European sailors sought a new trade route to Asia and stumbled onto these two continents thousands of years later.

Colonization Needed the Doctrine of Discovery

Why did Europe need to explore the world right at that point in time? For centuries, the Silk Road had been the trade route from West to East and vice versa. Things changed in the 1400s.

That's when things got complicated during the Ottoman Empire. Istanbul was Constantinople, now it's Istanbul, not Constantinople. Why did Constantinople get the works?

That little avenue between Europe and Asia was conquered by the Ottoman Turks in 1453, making travel along the Silk Road a challenge for European traders who had up until then relied on safe passage without usurious tariffs or danger of political instability. Piracy and violence became more commonplace. There must be another way to get to all those lucrative Asian goods beyond Turkey.

That is why Columbus was looking for a better path to India. Who knew India was a ridiculous number of miles away if you traveled in the opposite direction from the Silk Road? Not Columbus or his benefactors, clearly.

The Doctrine of Discovery

By the mid-1400s, the Portuguese were trading in and around the African continent and engaging in the slave trade. Later in the century, Christopher Columbus made his voyage to what he thought would be India but wound up on an island called Guanahani in what we now call the Bahamas. He saw land and people ripe for exploiting. Neither the Portuguese slave trade nor Columbus stumbling onto Guanahani were problematic for the leaders sending these explorers and merchants. The Church had their backs.

What do I mean by this? Two papal bulls (edicts) helped pave the way for the okey-dokey on African slave trade and the conquest of the Americas and other non-European parts of the world. First, Pope Nicholas V issued *Romanus Pontifex* in 1455.[4] This gave the Portuguese a monopoly on trade in Africa and authorized enslaving Africans. Then, as exploration gained steam in North America, Pope Alexander VI issued *Inter Caetera* in 1493, granting official ownership of the New World to Ferdinand and Isabella, king and queen of Spain. To these monarchs, the pope declared:[5]

> *"We of our own motion, and not at your solicitation, do give, concede, and assign for ever to you and your successors, all the islands, and main lands,*

---

[4] Christian Aboriginal Infrastructure Developments. *The Bull Romanus Pontifex (Nicholas V), January 8, 1455*
[5] (Papal Encyclicals Online)

discovered; and which may hereafter, be discovered, towards the west and south; whether they be situated towards India, or towards any other part whatsoever, and give you absolute power in them."

This was used as a justification for European explorers to claim lands for the nations they represented. The *Inter Caetera* was broadly used as the justification for colonization and conquest in Africa, Asia, Australia, and New Zealand as well as the Americas.

While the Doctrine of Discovery is more than these two pronouncements, they laid the foundation for what was to come.

Explorers and the nations they represented needed to justify grabbing land from people who already occupied that land. This is not unique, in that wars and conflict since the beginning of time tend to revolve around grabbing disputed land. It was the breadth and scope of the land grab here that was a completely new set of circumstances. And, up to this point, land was most often grabbed by people who looked like you but had a different leader, one at odds with your leader. A land grab of this magnitude was not your average spoils of war.

The second justification needed was for enslaving people. Again, nothing new about enslaving your enemies. But the breadth and scope were going to become something different entirely.

The roots of the concept of race can be traced to the need to justify colonization and enslavement. Ta-Nehisi Coates says it so well in a September 2020 *Vanity Fair* article[6]: "In order to plunder a people of everything, you must plunder their humanity first."

So, in the 1400s, Europeans found there was a big, wide world out there that was ripe for conquest. There were political and economic forces at work that compelled the exploration and exploitation of these already-inhabited lands in Africa and the Americas.

---

[6] Coates, Ta-Nehisi. "Ta-Nehisi Coates on Black Lives Matter, Protests, and Editing Vanity Fair." *Vanity Fair*, 24 August 2020,

A Brief History of White Nonsense

Why was it okay to go on what would become, between the 1500s and 1800s, the biggest land grab in history? The justification became that European culture was simply superior and other groups of people were subhuman, needed the help and expertise of European culture, or, most often, both.

Tracing the justifications for "discovery" and enslavement takes us on a convoluted path. Building the ideas that would shape the identities of people from multiple continents didn't happen overnight. It was clear from the beginning that justification of White Nonsense often put religious institutions and political leaders in lockstep with one another. That's what happened as Europeans began exploring and then colonizing other parts of the world. Law professor Robert A. Williams, Jr. says:

> *Responding to the requirements of a paradoxical age of Renaissance and Inquisition, the West's first modern discourses of conquest articulated a vision of all humankind united under a rule of law discoverable solely by human reason. Unfortunately for the American Indian, the West's first tentative steps towards this noble vision of a Law of Nations contained a mandate for Europe's subjugation of all peoples whose radical divergence from European-derived norms of right conduct signified their need for conquest and remediation.* [7]

Understanding Today

The Doctrine of Discovery did not just stay neatly in the past. The point of this brief book is to look at the throughlines that brought us to today. Colonization justified by the Doctrine of Discovery led

---

[7] *Williams, Robert A., Jr. 1992.* The American Indian in Western Legal Thought: The Discourses of Conquest. *Oxford: Oxford University Press, p. 59, in Dunbar-Ortiz, Roxanne. 2015.* An Indigenous Peoples' History of the United States. *Boston: Beacon Press, pp. 3–4.*

A Brief History of White Nonsense

Europeans to develop the concept of race and put themselves at the top of this newly invented hierarchy.

In delving briefly into the plain, unambiguous facts of history, we can step back and understand the world we're living in. And we can, hopefully, continue to reshape where we are going so that, in the words of teacher, activist, 2020 presidential candidate, and member of the Navajo Nation, Mark Charles: "'We the People' can finally mean All the People."[8]

Some of our kids are being taught this common history if they happen to have a class based on something like Howard Zinn's *A People's History*. But unless you are currently in grade school or just recently graduated from high school, you probably were not taught this common history, even though Zinn has been writing and providing resources on this subject for decades. And for current students, there is a major outcry from concerned white parents who do not want this history explored.

History has been too often whitewashed so "heroes" could remain unexamined. The full breadth of history has been shined up a bit so the mistakes made don't look so bad.

In fact, as you can imagine, there is an active movement in opposition to sharing these plain facts of history. As I write this, there is a concerted effort to elect school board members who will stamp out "Critical Race Theory" in public elementary and high schools and even stop Diversity, Equity, and Inclusion initiatives in schools. I wasn't taught Critical Race Theory, and neither are your school-age children being taught it; it is taught in law schools and certain college classes. It's a very specific academic theory about the effects of racism.

---

[8] Charles uses this language in much of his public speaking, and notably in his co-authored book with Soong-Chan Rah, *Unsettling Truths: the Ongoing, Dehumanizing Legacy of the Doctrine of Discovery*, Downers Grove, InterVarsity Press, 2019.

Some parents are scared of real history, and they are inventing excuses for not teaching children the unambiguous facts of history. But if kids are old enough to learn about Anne Frank, they are old enough to hear about our whole history and perhaps step out of the White Nonsense that has stunted our nation up to this point.

A straightforward look at history is needed so we can understand where we've come from and how to move forward into a racism-free future.

I was in my 40s when I first learned about the Doctrine of Discovery. An honest history would have this concept taught in our public education system.

But some are fearful of this kind of clear and open airing of the history of the US, to the point of calling it "Anti-American." Some call attempts at a full airing of history "revisionist." Revising what we know of history to include the full breadth of what has happened should not be demonized. So maybe this is "revisionist" history, but in order to understand where we've been, we need to know these things. If that is revisionist, I'll wear it as a badge of honor.

The Roots of Racism Are Dehumanization

I find it interesting that in these early days of White Nonsense, Europeans had enough awareness of what they were doing—exploiting land and people—that they felt justification for this behavior was needed and even required. In order to excuse this exploitative behavior, the humans they met along the way would need to be "downgraded." They would need to be dehumanized.

The important thing to understand is that racism was the outgrowth—the needed justification—for the actions taken by the colonizers. Racism was not the precursor of this era, but the cancerous outgrowth. Hope College's "Getting Race Right" blog says it well:

A Brief History of White Nonsense

Most of us assume that racism led to the conquest of American Natives and to the enslavement of Africans. Cox, Fredrickson, and many others argue just the opposite: that conquest and slavery led to racism because of the need to justify what was being done. The idea of race as a fundamental difference among people groups was buttressed over the centuries as Europeans and their descendants continued to rule over other parts of the world. "Race" became a distinctive, and especially powerful, means of organizing a world view necessary to justify the social, political, and economic order of colonialism.[9]

I agree with this assessment. Slave trade in Europe began with the Portuguese, who were interested in gaining a foothold with traders in Morocco. In 1444, Prince Henry of Portugal held a slave auction. This was around the same time the Genoese in Italy and Valencians in Spain were starting to engage in the sale of African captives, according to Ibram X. Kendi in his book, *Stamped from the Beginning*[10]. Just a few years later, colonization of the Americas would begin.

In order for good "Christian" Europeans to justify the conquest they were undertaking, they needed to define non-Europeans as something else. They needed to establish something beyond US vs. THEM. They needed to create an OTHER.

Since European powers used the Doctrine of Discovery as the legal and moral basis for exploring and taking land in the name of Portugal, Spain, England, etc., it is no surprise that colonial governments, including the English colonies that would form the initial 13 united states, wrote the Doctrine of Discovery into laws in those jurisdictions as well.

---

[9] Hope College. "How did the idea of race develop? - Getting Race Right." *Hope College Blog Network*

[10] Kendi, Ibram X. *Stamped from the Beginning: The Definitive History of Racist Ideas in America*. PublicAffairs, 2016

The Doctrine of Discovery and the invention of a supposed racial hierarchy created a problem so pernicious that its tendrils, like a weed that creates a warren of interlocking roots below ground, cannot be easily removed, and continues to grow. That weed is persistently popping up today.

The Doctrine of Discovery is the starting point of that root system. It is the reason why, 100 years after the Civil War and a few amendments to the Constitution ended slavery and gave African American men the right to vote, a civil rights struggle still remained in the 1960s. It is why, even though redlining was outlawed (though just in my lifetime), so many neighborhoods are still segregated by race. It is why Native culture is so often treated like a caricature or historic artifact instead of a present reality.

The Doctrine of Discovery as a legal concept has been used throughout our history to justify shortchanging Native American interests and putting the dominant culture's interests ahead. The US Supreme Court cited a Doctrine of Discovery precedent as recently as 2005 in *City of Sherrill v. Oneida Nation*.[11] None other than progressive stalwart Justice Ruth Bader Ginsberg authored the majority opinion in that case.

White Nonsense, rooted in the Doctrine of Discovery and the fiction of race, has rippled through history from Columbus to today. Here are just a few of the throughlines.

1492–1619: European Colonization Begins

With justifications in place, the land grab and human exploitation could begin in earnest. As discovery quickly led to conquest, we see justification in full force, as well as a measure of skepticism and even horror at the way Native people were treated

---

[11] United States Department of Justice. "City of Sherrill v. Oneida Indian Nation NY - Amicus (Merits)." *Department of Justice*, 21 October 2014

when European explorers "discovered" them living their lives. These two impulses are exemplified in the lives of Christopher Columbus and Bartolome de las Casas. One had nations and regions named after him, the other has been relegated for most of history to a curiosity delved into by college history geeks.

Let's look at these two counterpoints in the early days of colonization.

Christopher Columbus

Writing about what Christopher Columbus actually said and did is revisionism of the most necessary order. He said what he said and did what he did in the name of God and King (and Queen), and a lot of it was pretty ugly.

For our purposes, there's no need to go into exhaustive detail about the voyages to the "new world" that Columbus led. But here are some White Nonsense highlights.

Columbus immediately saw the economic upside of subjugating and enslaving the people he found. The *Inter Caetera* was his justification for claiming the land for Spain, kidnapping residents of the islands, enslaving them and forcing them to "convert" to Christianity[12]. Jesus, Mary, and Joseph, this is how all this nonsense started!

The united interests of church and state were clear from the beginning of White Nonsense. Beginning in 1514, Spanish conquerors adopted the *Requirement*, an ultimatum in which Indigenous people were forced to accept "the Church as the Ruler and Superior of the whole world" or face persecution. If Indigenous people did not immediately comply, the *Requirement*[13] warned them:

---

[12] (History.com)
[13] National Humanities Center. "The Requerimiento [Requirement], Council of Castile, 1510

We shall take you and your wives and your children, and shall make slaves of them, and as such shall sell and dispose of them as their Highnesses may command; and we shall take away your goods, and shall do all the harm and damage that we can.

Often the Requirement was read to Indigenous people without translation, in some cases even from ships before crew members landed to kill Indigenous people and take captives for slavery.

Yet these days, the legacy of Columbus is showing signs of wear. More and more communities and states are opting to celebrate Indigenous People's Day rather than Columbus Day, for instance. Commemorative statues are being torn down, and his role in propagating the Doctrine of Discovery like a virus—, along with spreading literal viruses, —is becoming part of the common narrative.

"Benevolent" Colonization – Bartolome de las Casas

In some ways, he was the anti-Columbus. De las Casas saw the plunder of people in the world Columbus had stumbled upon and was horrified. While popes and heads of state worked out how to legitimize the plunder, Bartolome de las Casas—part of the Catholic Dominican Order—worked to document the horror and create a more benevolent approach to White Nonsense.

The life and work of de las Casas and his canonization as a saint (even while the slaughter of Native people continued) shows us that some saw the horror and destructive potential of White Nonsense from the beginning.

Yet, here we must contend with the two forms of racism we will see expressed over and over in the kudzu-like growth of White Nonsense. There is the violent and overt racism exemplified from the very beginning by people like Columbus. And there is the gentler, paternalistic racism of people like de las Casas, who saw Native people as in need of a "protector." This literally became the title by which de las Casas was known, given by Cardinal Cisneros.

Being nice is certainly better than wholesale slaughter, but let's not give de las Casas a pass here. The roots of ethnic superiority of Europeans are still present in his actions. He sought colonization through less-violent means, but he still saw Turtle Island as a land Europeans could and should "civilize."

Throughline: Resistance in the Age of Colonization

I recently moved to New Mexico, where there are long-standing, vibrant Native communities. Literally thousands of years of vibrancy. This is, after all, where Clovis Culture got its name for the unique spearheads used by hunters 13,000-ish years ago.

But on to more recent history. First contact with European invaders happened around 1540, when Spanish explorers were looking for the Seven Cities of Gold, which of course did not exist. What they did find, according to *The Heartbeat of Wounded Knee*[14] author David Treuer, was "a well-populated, well-demarcated...homeland that had been settled for millennia by constantly evolving tribal groups, among them the Diné, Tewa (who themselves included the Zuni, Acoma, Cochiti, Taos, and more), Pima, O'odham, and Apache."

The history of White Nonsense is not a history of people of color sitting back and letting stuff just happen. By the mid-1600s, the Pueblo people were weary of the treatment they were receiving at the hands of the Spanish.[15]

---

[14] (Treuer p. 140)
[15] Ortiz Simon J et al. Po'pay : Leader of the First American Revolution. 1st ed. Clear Light Pub 2005.

Po'pay and the Pueblo Rebellion

In what is now northern and central New Mexico, the Tewa (referred to collectively as Pueblo) people had been living and doing their thing for centuries. Along came the Spanish, imposing their European religious, economic, and political ideas on people who had been doing just fine. Even today, the longest continuously inhabited group of homes in North America are located at the historic Taos Pueblo.

In 1680, tensions came to a head after the Spanish governor ordered the deaths of several Pueblo holy men. Some were whipped in public as a warning to others. Po'Pay was a leader who was whipped in the square in Santa Fe. This act became a last straw. Po'Pay of Ohkay Owingeh (which the colonizers called San Juan Pueblo) led a coordinated armed rebellion. A date was set, and runners were sent to all of the Pueblos with news of the exact day when the rebellion would begin. The revolt was such a success that it curtailed Spanish rule in the Pueblo region for 12 years.

After the rebellion, the Spanish conceded on several points to the Pueblo people, allowing them to remain on Pueblo lands, preserve a level of autonomy, and develop a process for lodging grievances with the colonial government.

To this day, Pueblos hold running events in part to commemorate the runners who spread the word about the 1680 Pueblo revolt.

Resistance has been a part of the history of colonized North America since the beginning. How did the Native people where you live resist White Nonsense from the earliest days?

Discovery Needed the Invention of "Race"

Claims of "discovery" are a piece of the White Nonsense puzzle. But beyond legal justifications for taking other people's land, an even more pernicious and destructive concept was born during this time period: the concept of *race*.

Curse of Ham

The concept of race did not arise out of thin air in the 1500s. Prior to the Doctrine of Discovery, there were other attempts by light-skinned people to dehumanize dark-skinned people. Often, religion was used as a justifying force.

The <u>Curse of Ham</u>[16] is one example. Over the centuries, the story of Noah's curse of his son Ham has been used to marginalize many groups of people. It was a handy trope for antisemitism, or anyone you wanted to marginalize. As colonialism took root, so did the notion that Africans were the descendants of Ham, somehow. With the invention of race, they could be considered a cursed race. Neat. Convenient. And, of course, complete religious nonsense.

The Concept of Race Matures

In the age of Enlightenment, perhaps the curse of Ham was not "scientific" enough. In order to make sense (and make permanent the taking of land and taking of freedom), those being treated this way needed to be put into a category, or categories, that made them literally less than human. This is how the invention of race happened.

This is the most important concept to understand as we move through post-Columbian history. Because, you see, the "white" in White Nonsense is pure fabrication. The invention of racial categories

---

[16] Lee, Felicia R. "From Noah's Curse to Slavery's Rationale." *The New York Times*, 1 November 2003

is pure nonsense but very necessary in perpetuating the social hierarchy, as the Doctrine of Discovery demands.

At its heart, White Nonsense is about the invention of the concept of race as the justification for dehumanizing and enslaving other human beings on a mass scale—not just spoils of war, but creating a whole goddamned economy based on the concept.

How did "Christian" Europe create this monstrous evil? "Whiteness" evolved over time. Uncoincidentally, the use of the term started in the early 1500s[17] and grew from describing aristocratic English women (whose skin was such because they were people of leisure who had no need to toil or do anything at all in the sun.) It then encompassed Anglo-Saxons (Northern and Western Europeans). Eventually, the term was used for all people of European descent.

Colonizers used the word "white" to refer to themselves, and the concept of race grew out of this reference. There is no way to understand the United States without putting the concept of race in the center. From English, Spanish, and French colonists to the US Founders and beyond, "whiteness" continued to evolve to include a wider range of people beyond Anglo-Saxon, but it was always meant to exclude and dehumanize people of African descent and Native people.

Pseudoscience and the Justification of White Nonsense

David R. Roediger, author and Foundation Distinguished Professor of American Studies and History at the University of Kansas, is quoted[18] as saying, "The world got along without race for

---

[17] Wiencek, Henry. "Historical Foundations of Race." *National Museum of African American History and Culture*
[18] (Wiencek)

the overwhelming majority of its history. The U.S. has never been without it."

Pseudoscientific justifications of the lie of white superiority were embraced by European settlers in the New (to them) World, and we will see in the following chapter how the lie of white supremacy made its way into the very fabric of the nation. A nation born out of very narrow notions of freedom and equality saw those notions expand over the intervening centuries, but we will also see how ideas baked into founding documents are hard to amend.

The Göttingen School

By the mid-1700s, biological superiority of Europeans was explored and explained as a scientific fact, most notably out of the University of Göttingen, where a group of German historians created terms for categorizing groups of people. The concepts developed by the Göttingen School remained in use well into the 20th century. Germans, amiright? Just kidding. This nonsense may have been hatched in Göttingen, but it got a big thumbs-up from people who considered themselves white all around Europe and into the Western Hemisphere.

The most notable figures in the Göttingen school were Johann Friedrich Blumenbach and Christoph Meiners[19] who developed a color terminology for the races they created: there was the Caucasian or white race; Mongolian or yellow race; Malayan or brown race; Ethiopian or black race; and American or red race.

Meiners made a study of physical, mental, and moral characteristics of each race. No surprise that his evidence produced a racial hierarchy with his race, the Caucasians, right at the top. Shocking. And while science and the work of anti-racists have thoroughly

---

[19] Bhopal, Raj, and John Usher. "The beautiful skull and Blumenbach's errors: the birth of the scientific concept of race." *NCBI*

debunked these notions, you will see different versions of racial hierarchy cropping up to justify current disparities in income, health outcomes, life expectancy, and more.

But the real, actual reasons for these discrepancies boil down to the fact that the throughlines of White Nonsense remain strong and the desire to keep the racial hierarchy intact is powerful. Strap in, because this is when White Nonsense goes into overdrive.

Drapetomania

Another pseudoscience that became popular during the era when chattel slavery was legal in the US was Drapetomania. Guess what happens when you enslave people? They want to get the hell out of that situation. But White Nonsense dictated that Africans were "suited to servitude."

Physician Samuel Cartwright came up with a rationale for the "strange behavior" of trying to escape the natural order of chattel slavery: it was a mental disorder. He wrote, "the Negro is a slave by nature and can never be happy...in any other condition."[20] So, behavior out of sync with servitude was to be viewed as abnormal. Ideas don't get much more repugnant than that, yet 170+ years later versions of this argument are made in microaggressions, or comments on social media. This absolute nonsense survives.

Cartwright presented this idea in 1851 at a meeting of the Louisiana Medical Association. He invented the term Drapetomania, derived from the Greek words for "runaway slave" and "crazy." (Commence eyerolls, please.) This guy was something. He went even further with this absurd idea, suggesting that enslavers who treated enslaved people as "equals" (an idea that in itself is a troubling notion, given the power dynamic; if one person owns another, there is no

---

[20] Equal Justice Initiative. "Mar. 17, 1851 | Pro-Slavery Doctor Calls Enslaved People's Desire to Be Free 'Curable Mental Disease.'"

equality) would trigger the disease. Not surprisingly, treatments for this "curable mental disease" included amputation of toes and severe whipping. Very original, Dr. Cartwright.

And again, while most of us can see these ideas as ludicrous, the echoes of Drapetomania can be heard in the modern world. For instance, when I was younger there were not many African American quarterbacks in the NFL. I heard serious discussions that this was because they lacked the intellect and leadership skills to lead teams to victory. Wow.

Francis Galton and the Roots of Eugenics

Drapetomania might not be in your everyday lexicon, but you may well have heard the term *eugenics* before. White Nonsense can present itself in a lot of different ways. The Civil War did not stop white people from wondering, "Are we genetically superior to these people we enslaved?" Even if slavery came to be seen as an appalling institution, there must be a reason those people "let themselves" be enslaved.

The disturbing pseudoscience of racial superiority was blossoming during this period.

In the late 1800s, fear of a Black Planet was on the rise among scared white people. Fears of "race degeneration" through racial mixing, people of color having more children, and even lower-class whites having more children led a British mathematician to devise a field of pseudoscience of which "race betterment" was the goal.

Galton called this concept "eugenics" from the Greek, meaning "noble in heredity." The ultimate goal was to breed people with desirable hereditary traits and discourage less desirable hereditary lines from continuing. Unfortunately, his cognitive testing found that the poor scored as well as their "betters."

With White Nonsense—that is, the presupposition that white people are inherently superior—eugenics took some very nasty turns.

One of the most famous proponents in the United States was President Theodore Roosevelt, who warned that the failure of couples of Anglo-Saxon heritage to produce large families would lead to "race suicide."[21]

Racial Integrity Act of 1924

The idea of racial purity became more and more popular following the Civil War. Overt white supremacy is (mostly) thought of today as a fringe movement. But in the early 20th century, this shit was totally mainstream, from the White House to the world of commerce. In 1914, J.H. Kellogg sponsored the first Race Betterment Conference.[22]

Attendees included Harry H. Laughlin, who proposed sterilization laws to keep "undesirable traits" from continuing through the generations.

Eugenics became mainstream social science as well in the early 20th century. It was challenged, but the ideas of one group being "advanced" and others "backwards" was common.

The Bell Curve, Shelby Steele, and Other Apologists for White Nonsense

White Nonsense does not just stay neatly in the past. *The Bell Curve*[23] was written in 1994 by Charles Murray and Richard J. Herrnstein. Interest in the book has grown in recent years, as has the controversy over the book's presentation of findings regarding IQ and

---

[21] Miller, George. "Teddy Roosevelt and Race Suicide." *Postcard History*, 7 February 2022

[22] Leung, Colette. "Race Betterment Foundation - Connections - Eugenics Archives."

[23] Murray, Charles, and Richard J. Herrnstein. *The bell curve*. Free Press, 1996.

race. The authors present data showing lower IQ scores of African Americans compared with European Americans. What the book does not address is why these findings are of interest to the authors. The book does not delve into potential reasons beyond race for this disparity. Readers are left with a de facto argument for the racial superiority of whites, with no context regarding historic bias in IQ testing or other factors that easily explain the data.

From the origins of the concept of race through today, there has always been a cottage industry of well-credentialed academics explaining that either white racial superiority is a simple fact or that, whatever the data suggest, systemic racism is not to blame. Wondering why White Nonsense persists? The need for justifications—no matter how much mental gymnastics it requires—for the persistent white foothold on power.

This is definitely one school of thought with plenty of supporters. I find their arguments lacking, and I believe that the key to a future multiethnic society requires a clear-eyed understanding of exactly this kind of White Nonsense and the problems it has wrought.

I started reading essays by Shelby Steele in college, when I read the Lewis Lapham-helmed *Harper's Magazine*. The magazine was my go-to for "limousine liberal" thought. Steele sees liberalism, not systemic racism, as the main roadblock to racial justice.

Steele is a Black intellectual, and author of many books, including *White Guilt: How Blacks and Whites Together Destroyed the Promise of the Civil Rights Era*.[24] (How "Blacks" destroyed that promise? Yikes!). He is currently a Robert J. and Marion E. Oster Senior Fellow at Stanford University's Hoover Institution, a notable conservative think-tank.

I was surprised when I found Steele so often featured, and surprised that I had so many problems with his assumptions of the

---

[24] Steele, Shelby. *White Guilt*. HarperCollins, 2007

basics of racism in the US. Steele is an African American writer and scholar serving as a senior fellow at the Hoover Institution.

Attending an anti-racism training event, I approached the group of facilitators. "I've been reading Shelby Steele..." I began. I later learned that the facilitators were apprehensive about where I was going with my question. Because they, like me, had some serious problems with Shelby Steele.

Steele and younger Black counterparts like James McWhorter seem to see anti-racism as a tool to simply make white people feel guilty and people of color feel like victims. And let me add fuel to the fire by saying here, I really don't understand how McWhorter, an Ivy League professor of linguistics, can have such a narrow (read: wrong) definition of anti-racism. Because understanding history—gaining a clear perception of the world we live in—isn't about either white guilt or global-majority victimhood. It requires being clear-eyed about the roadblocks we all face together and finding a path beyond them.

Let's argue about where we go from here, with "conservative" and "liberal" ideas vying for a position that leads to concrete action when it comes to ending racism and the White Nonsense that props it up. What is not up for debate—and this is the whole of my argument in this book—are the unambiguous facts of history that led us here.

Moving Beyond the Nonsense

In propping up whiteness since the days of "discovery," we as a society are not getting at the root of the imperfection of our union.

I'm not here to pretend there are simple fixes to this problem. Theft of personhood, property, and land that occurs over multiple generations cannot be easily unwound. And we will see over the course of this history that when attempted solutions are based on some of the same foundational lies that started the whole mess, and when the perpetrators of the nonsense are alone put in charge of creating those solutions, they often turn into half-measures. So, for example, when slavery was at long last abolished, former slaves were still treated as "less than" by the dominant white culture because of the lies perpetrated by White Nonsense.

The plain facts of history show that these original sins morph, the language used to justify the sin changes, but the questioning of certain people's personhood remains. That stuff does not just go away. We can't all "just get along" because the origins of the United States and the systems developed over time were developed with the purpose—sometimes overt and out in the open, sometimes just unconscious assumptions—of keeping white people at the top of the social hierarchy.

So, once Europeans meandered into the territories occupied by the Taino, Havasupai, Algonquin, Powhatan, and many others, the interactions were informed by a worldview on the part of Europeans that assumed they were meant to take the land and transfer their cultural norms to those places.

One big lesson to learn: beware when white people declare racism "solved." I hope as a nation that we can look back on our history and find that we did, collectively, find solutions to nullify the centuries-long impacts of White Nonsense. But in order to find solutions, we have to have a common understanding of our history. It's not pretty, it is chock-full of nonsense, but in order to face the future and find bold solutions, it is necessary work.

A Brief History of White Nonsense

Chapter 3
Throughline: Maintaining the Social Hierarchy of White Nonsense

With bedrock principles in place and expanded on over time, White Nonsense was given space and centuries to thrive. Once the fiction of race was developed as supposed fact, it needed to be justified and "proven" over time. So we see the language of supremacy in the wielding of colonial power, from Spain and Portugal in South and Central America, to the Dutch and English in eastern North America. We see the presupposition of supremacy in the language of our founding documents. We see the language of supremacy in the justifications of slavery and even in how slavery was ended—with reparations offered not to enslaved people but to enslavers! We see the outcomes of supremacy in the broken treaties made with every Indigenous community in North America. We see the language of supremacy in the Jim Crow South and the equally segregated and redlined North. We see it in the overt terrorist acts of the KKK, and in the quiet lack of access to capital and in the white flight from cities to suburbs in the mid-20th century.

Why are we still dealing with racial divisions well into the 21st century? Because White Nonsense has not yet been fully held accountable for its actions.

Putting the System in Systemic Racism

What do people mean when they talk about systemic racism? A coherent definition is challenging because we're talking about all of the systems of public and private life that were developed over the past centuries. We are the frogs in the kettle, not noticing that we have reached boiling point. We (white Americans) are the fish in the sea, breathing in an ocean we created to order our world. I write in part to help us come to a common understanding of how all these systems were developed with this fatal flaw.

The Doctrine of Discovery is a touchstone for systematizing white-skin privilege. Political entities like the nation-states that sent out the early European explorers needed the Doctrine to justify taking land from others. Enlightenment philosophers and religious thinkers like the Puritans put the Doctrine to the test, expanding on its premise to further enshrine white supremacy as the primary assumption of how things were in the age of European exploration.

The presupposition of Eurocentrism is embedded in our founding documents, and every political compromise that has come after it has reflected the dynamic of white power navigating to keep that power, frequently—especially in recent times—without even realizing it.

To bring things into the near-present for a few paragraphs, the crime bill of 1994 is a perfect example of this. So, Bill Clinton (you know, the "first Black president") put in place bipartisan "tough on crime" landmark legislation. It was likely a factor in the reduction of rates of violent crime, which had peaked in 1991. But the act's sentencing guidelines along with the Anti-Drug Abuse Act of 1986 meant significant disparities of sentencing between crack and powder cocaine, which led to an increase in mass incarceration of people of color. Many members of the Congressional Black Caucus joined in support of this bill, although some significant names did not, including Representatives John Lewis, Maxine Waters, John Conyers, and Charles Rangel.

That is just one example of how racist policies continue to cause problems in our experiment in democracy. Without a clear-eyed understanding of the roots of white supremacy, public policy and laws written centuries later are still dripping with the stuff. So let's take a closer look at how White Nonsense was infused into every aspect of US American society, from commerce to politics to social interactions of every kind. Let's look at how the social hierarchy of White Nonsense was and is maintained.

Transatlantic Slave Trade Begins

There's no talking about White Nonsense without an exploration of the slave trade. The important thing to reiterate is that White Nonsense does not begin and end with slavery. Racism in the US didn't come out of nowhere in 1619 and just come to a sudden end in 1865. Far from it.

Here is how the invention of whiteness aided and abetted the enslavement of Africans. In 1526, a year after the Protestant Reformation began when Martin Luther posted his 95 Theses on the cathedral door in Wittenberg, Germany, a Portuguese trading ship–with a cargo that included enslaved Africans–completed its first voyage to Brazil. Other European countries soon took this as the go-ahead for enslaving Africans and putting them to work in these worlds they were "discovering."

Good Catholics and Protestants alike soon used the Doctrine of Discovery and a reading of the New Testament that ignored the Sermon on the Mount but paid homage to the "slaves obey your masters" bits from Paul. Yay, Jesus wants me for an enslaver!

This was also the era when, along with people like de las Casas, some white people began to see the nonsense of this path. But through the Doctrine of Discovery and the invention of "race," white supremacy was born and began to flourish. Slavery and subjugation won the day in the name of Christianizing and civilizing people who had lived and thrived in these lands, for tens of thousands of years in some cases.

In this early era, the slave trade primarily moved human beings to South America. The trade was dominated by Portugal and, to a lesser extent, Spain. This became known as the First Atlantic System. But the English wanted in on this action.

1619

The year 1619 is a watershed date in North American history. While slavery existed in South America and into New Spain (which, in the US at various points included lands from Florida through most of what is now the Western US) in the early days of colonization, English colonies on the eastern seaboard of the US began engaging in the slave trade in August of 1619, when a slave ship arrived in Point Comfort, now Fort Monroe, in what was then the Virginia Territory.

Between 20 and 30 humans were traded from the *White Lion*, a British pirate vessel that had captured them from a Portuguese ship called the *São João Bautista*. They were traded for provisions and the *White Lion* went on its way. The human beings were technically indentured servants at that point, but that was only because Virginia had not yet established laws regarding slavery.

Among the group of human beings forcibly taken from their homes and sold as cargo in Point Comfort were a couple known as Anthony and Isabella. Their son, William Tucker, was born in Jamestown in 1624 as the first person of African ancestry born in the 13 British colonies. We don't know much about William's life other than that he, like his parents, was technically an indentured servant.

European colonists would need to quickly codify their nonsense to prevent servants of African descent from thinking they could gain their freedom after a set number of years, as their poor European-descended counterparts did.

Throughline: Resistance
Elizabeth Key Grinstead

On July 21, 1656, Elizabeth Key Grinstead[25] sued the colony of Virginia and won freedom for herself and her infant son, John Grinstead II. Elizabeth was born in 1630 just 11 years after the first Africans were brought to the English colonies in North America. She was born to an African woman who was named Martha by her enslaver (technically she was an indentured servant, as laws regarding slavery were not yet codified in Virginia). Martha's enslaver, Thomas Key, was a white tobacco planter who was eventually elected to the Virginia House of Burgesses. You guessed it, Key was married and Martha was enslaved, so this was no innocent tryst between consenting adults. This was a rape by a person in power against a person he exerted power over. That's the reality Elizabeth was born into.

Without White Nonsense—that is, the invention of race and the arbitrary and unfactual classification of the white "race" as superior—Elizabeth would have served a term of indentured servitude as was required of "illegitimate" children of the time. She should have been freed from servitude in 1645 but had been passed along to several landowners in the intervening years. She eventually was placed with a man named John Mottram. When Mottram died in 1655, his children tried to reclassify Elizabeth and her son John as Negro slaves—property of the estate, according to Virginia law that had by then figured out how to do race-based slavery. Her claim of freedom was based on the fact that her father was an Englishman and she was baptized a Christian. Whatever it takes, Elizabeth. Good for you!

---

[25] Robinson, Yonaia. Elizabeth Key Grinstead (1630–1665) • 21 June 2021, www.blackpast.org/african-american-history/grinstead-elizabeth-key-1630.

Without a white English father, Elizabeth and young John would have been shit out of luck. But because in English common law the legal status of the father determined the status of the children, Elizabeth was, at 25 years of age, finally granted freedom from what was supposed to be seven years of indentured servitude.

Elizabeth Key Grinstead kind of slipped through the cracks in the early days of White Nonsense. In later years, the offspring of rape victims on plantations would be bought and sold just like any other enslaved person. In fact, it became a means of perpetuating enslavement from generation to generation.

That Time African Medicine Saved Colonizer Lives: Onesimus and Inoculation Against Smallpox

While the Virginia colony was figuring out how to codify enslavement of persons of African descent, the Puritans were doing their thing up in the Massachusetts colony. Same White Nonsense, different context.

Among the enslaved human beings up north was a man named Onesimus.[26] His story is an example of the contributions of African Americans to US history cannot be limited to the wealth created via free forced labor. Since the beginning, African Americans have made contributions in every area of society. Let's take medicine for example.

Massachusetts colonial Cotton Mather has a certain notoriety in early American history for having presided over the Salem witchcraft trials. But there is another story with a Cotton Mather connection that is worth learning about.

Onesimus was a human being gifted by a Christian congregation to their pastor, Cotton Mather. I know, holy crap! We know him as Onesimus because Mather named this grown human

---

[26] Nielsen, Euell A. "Onesimus (?- ?) •." *Blackpast*, 3 June 2020

being after a slave mentioned in the Bible, which makes it totally okay. (Hint: no, it does not.)

Mather taught Onesimus to read and write English, provided a home, and allowed (allowed!) him to have a family. All this to say, this human owned by another human was offered a level of autonomy that most other owned humans were not afforded.

In 1716, smallpox was raging through the Massachusetts colony and elsewhere in the 13 British colonies. Mather asked Onesimus about any experience he might have had where he grew up, most likely in the region of West Africa we now know as Ghana. Onesimus described a sort of inoculation process where the puss of a person infected with smallpox was rubbed into the open wound of a noninfected person. The result, as anyone from that region of the world would tell you, was that the recipient would be immune from smallpox.

Mather was interested in having this practice tested in New England, but the medical community was reluctant to trust traditional remedies recommended by an enslaved African. Yet, during an outbreak of smallpox in 1721, a physician, an uncle of John Adams, took an interest in this process Mather had told him about. He used the process with 242 patients, with only six resulting deaths. Onesimus's method became the standard for inoculation against smallpox.

So an enslaved human brought an inoculation for smallpox to the colonizers. This is just one example of how people regarded by White Nonsense as "less than" made contributions with a huge impact on the world, then and now.

Throughline: Resistance – Armed Rebellion Against White Nonsense

Resistance to slavery came in many forms, starting all the way back in the 1600s. From theft and work disruption to running away.

Open, organized rebellion against enslavement happened as well. Numerous rebellions occurred throughout the Americas during the early colonial period and in the first century of the existence of the United States. Here are just a few of those that occurred in North America[27]:

- *Gloucester County, Virginia, 1663* – a rebellion of enslaved Africans and Irish, Native, and English indentured servants
- *New York Slave Revolt of 1712* – a revolt of 23 enslaved Africans
- *Samba Rebellion of 1731* – a revolt in what was then French Louisiana led by an enslaved African man known to history as Samba Bambara
- *Gabriel's Rebellion of 1800* – enslaved Virginia blacksmith Gabriel Prosser planned a large revolt that was foiled before it started
- *Black Seminole Slave Rebellion of 1835–38* – Native and Black Seminoles fought the US Army in Florida

The most successful slave revolt happened in the nearby Bahamas when the ship *The Creole* was taken over by enslaved people, freeing 128.

---

[27] Blakemore, Erin. "How two centuries of slave revolts shaped American history." *National Geographic*, 8 November 2019

White Nonsense in the Founding Documents

In order to understand where we are right now, we have to dig in and see how the Doctrine of Discovery and the pseudoscience of race led to melanin deficiency becoming a false marker of racial superiority.

Since the beginning of the republic, Indigenous people and people of African descent have made massive contributions, from the formation of democracy itself to advances in medicine, industry, and so much more. Yet newcomers of European descent formed governments and other systems predicated on false beliefs about white supremacy.

The history of North America up to this point shows the colonization of this continent by European settlers was part of the larger movement of colonization and exploitation that European nations (particularly Spain, Portugal, the Netherlands, England, and France, but many others as well) carried out throughout the Americas, Africa, and Asia. They really thought highly of themselves.

US history tends to focus on English colonization because that is who the original US colonies broke away from, but the colonization of the Americas was done by many European nation-states.

With colonization in North America based on the lie of white supremacy, it is no surprise at all that the founding documents of the United States have the basic flaw of white supremacy written right into them. That's not me being mean or wanting people who identify as white to feel bad. It is a simple, unambiguous fact of history.

In many ways, the founding documents have stood us in good stead. These documents and the nation they created have stood the test of time.

But when it comes to promoting the fiction of race, our desire to form a more perfect union should compel us to look carefully at these documents, understand the overtly racist components, and do what is necessary to correct these false assumptions.

A Brief History of White Nonsense

Overt presence of the language of racial hierarchy is why social scientists and historians talk about "systemic racism." Because this shit was baked in from the beginning. I do not write these words with any joy or glibness. I have grown up with a profound respect for the longevity, flexibility, and adaptability of our founding documents, particularly the Constitution. But as we will see, the historical record is clear and unambiguous. The presupposition of white supremacy is overt and present, even as a more perfect multicultural union was sought and fought for over centuries.

You might wonder, how could the Founding Fathers sign their names to a document declaring that "All Men Are Created Equal" while enslaving people? How could they, when forming a permanent government at the Constitutional Convention, call humans from Africa three-fifths of a person? How could the founders write into the Declaration itself a description of other humans as "savages"? The original inhabitants of North America are people who had created a mosaic of cultures, languages, and ways of being loooooong before Europeans had the wherewithal to cross the ocean and find already-inhabited land. How could this happen?

Well, save your cognitive dissonance for another time, because the answer is the Doctrine of Discovery and all those other justifications for dehumanizing thoughts and behaviors that brought us to this point. By removing full humanity from the equation, freedom and equality became relative terms.

Once the 13 colonies had gained independence from Britain, there was some handwringing about the institution of slavery, especially as they evolved from a loose federation of states into a nation called the United States.

Was slavery universally embraced in the colonial era? No. Were there abolitionists who saw the irony in the talk of freedom and equality limited largely to landowning white men? Yes. But slavery was such a big part of the economic engine of this young nation that the founders learned to make peace with the idea precisely because of the presumption of white supremacy.

The prior centuries had made the fiction of white superiority a common understanding among European colonizers. It was an underlying condition of the founding of the United States, as our founding documents unambiguously show.

Declaration of Independence

Digging into the texts of our founding documents, the white supremacy invented out of whole cloth over the previous two centuries is in plain view.

There are the obvious statements, like "we hold these truths to be self-evident, that all men are created equal." "Men" of course meant white landowning men.

As we read further in the Declaration of the many grievances the colonists had against King George, we see more evidence of White Nonsense in the mention of the original occupants of the land the colonies claimed as their own: "He has excited domestic insurrections amongst us, and has endeavored to bring on the inhabitants of our frontiers, *the merciless Indian Savages*, whose known rule of warfare is an undistinguished destruction of all ages, sexes and conditions." (italics added)

The document calls the King "unfit to be the ruler of a free people," even as signers of the document literally engaged in human trafficking. The Doctrine of Discovery gave cover for Native humans and humans from Africa to be considered something less than "free people."

Iroquois Confederation

As the nation in its infancy was trying to form a more perfect union than the brutal, endless wars and disunity the colonizers had left in Europe, they took inspiration from people whom they referred to as "savages". One such inspiration was the Iroquois Confederacy.

The Iroquois Confederacy[28] was originally comprised of five nations: the Kanienkehaka ("people of the flint country," who you may know as Mohawks), the Onondaga ("the people of the hills"), the Seneca ("the people of the big hill"), the Cayuga ("where they land the boats"), and the Oneida ("people of the standing stone"). These groups were later joined by the Tuscarora ("people of the shirt"), who moved into the neighborhood in the early 1700s.

The original five nations of the Iroquois formed this union back in the mid-1100s and were led by a person known as the Great Peacemaker.

This, not the United States, is known as the oldest participatory democracy on earth. In 1988, the US Congress recognized the influence of the Iroquois Confederation on the formation of the original 13 colonies that would become the United States.

United States Constitution

After the Revolutionary War was won (with the help of Black soldiers and Native American scouts), there was the period of the Articles of Confederation. That went on for less than 10 years and turned out to be a pretty hinky way to run things. Independent states doing their own thing was just too chaotic. So, in 1787, a Constitutional Convention was convened, with the Constitution ratified a year later in 1788.

The language of the Constitution can be as troubling as that of the Declaration, with rights and privileges staked out for a particular set of people and specifically and intentionally excluded from others.

---

[28] Hansen, Terri. "How the Iroquois Great Law of Peace Shaped U.S. Democracy | Native America." *PBS*, 17 December 2018

A Brief History of White Nonsense

Let's start with "We the People." I am a proud US citizen, glad that this nation was founded on ideals of liberty and equality. But, like many, I want "we the people" to fully include all the people.

I am not making an idle point here. The language of exclusion is clear in the document, and if we want to form a more perfect union, we need to come to terms with these exclusions and the problems with attempts to remedy them (especially, as we will see, in the Amendments 13–15 that followed the Civil War.)

Three-Fifths of a Person

Perhaps the most famous of the white supremacist language infused in the founding documents is the idea of three-fifths of a person. That's how the Constitution describes enslaved people.

How would a representative democracy work with classes of people that included free and enslaved? Here's how Article 1, Section 2 of the US Constitution puts it: "Representatives and direct Taxes shall be apportioned among the several States which may be included within this Union, according to their respective Numbers, which shall be determined by adding to the whole Number of free Persons, including those bound to Service for a Term of Years, and excluding Indians not taxed, three fifths of all other Persons." Let's see, we have free persons, indentured servant persons—those are full people. Indigenous persons not taxed don't get counted. Who's left? Enslaved people are "all other persons," just a bit less of a person than free, mostly white people. Free Black people were counted as a whole person. That's a nice compromise by the white slave-owning writers of the Constitution!

Native Americans are also mentioned in Article 1 when it comes to regulating "Commerce with foreign Nations, and among the several States, and with the Indian Tribes."

Section 2 of Article 4 provides that enslaved people would not be afforded free movement within and among the States of the United

A Brief History of White Nonsense

States: "No Person held to Service or Labour in one State, under the Laws thereof, escaping into another, shall, in Consequence of any Law or Regulation therein, be discharged from such Service or Labour, but shall be delivered up on Claim of the Party to whom such Service or Labour may be due."

It should be noted that in the following century, the Confederate States would find the US Constitution wanting in its white supremacy. In the "Cornerstone Speech,"[29] Alexander Stephens, vice president of the Confederate States, said:

> *The new constitution has put at rest, forever, all the agitating questions relating to our peculiar institution African slavery as it exists among us the proper status of the negro in our form of civilization. This was the immediate cause of the late rupture and present revolution. Jefferson, in his forecast, had anticipated this, as the "rock upon which the old Union would split." He was right. What was conjecture with him, is now a realized fact. But whether he fully comprehended the great truth upon which that rock stood and stands, may be doubted. The prevailing ideas entertained by him and most of the leading statesmen at the time of the formation of the old Constitution, were that the enslavement of the African was in violation of the laws of nature; that it was wrong in principle, socially, morally and politically. It was an evil they knew not well how to deal with, but the general opinion of the men of that day was that, somehow or other in the order of Providence, the institution would be evanescent and pass away....Those ideas, however, were fundamentally wrong. They rested upon the assumption of the equality of races. This was an error. It was a sandy foundation, and the government built upon it fell when the "storm came and the wind blew."*
>
> *Our new government is founded upon exactly the opposite idea; its foundations are laid, its corner-stone rests, upon the great truth that the*

---

[29] Blackpast. "(1861) Alexander H. Stephens, "Cornerstone Speech" •." *Blackpast*, 27 November 2012

negro is not equal to the white man; that slavery subordination to the superior race is his natural and normal condition. This, our new government, is the first, in the history of the world, based upon this great physical, philosophical, and moral truth. This truth has been slow in the process of its development, like all other truths in the various departments of science.

I would like to think that Stephens was right in his assertion that the founders assumed the equality of all races. But the words of the Constitution and the history before and after the Civil War tell a very different story. While there was clearly significant debate over slavery during the formation of the US Constitution, the fact that the institution remained and the language regarding how Africans should be enumerated (the 3/5ths person clause) show that the humanity of enslaved Africans was something "less than." Contrary to Stephen's words above, there was no original assumption of the equality of the races.

Doctrine of Discovery Codified into US Law

The US has never fully deconstructed the institutions that resulted from the Doctrine of Discovery or the other legal maneuvers European colonizers used to justify enslavement and attempts at genocide of people who they did not classify as "white."

For instance, in *Johnson v. McIntosh*[30], an 1823 US Supreme Court decision in which Chief Justice Marshall specifically invoked the Discovery Doctrine, the question came before the court: could private US citizens pay Native nations for land? The unanimous court decision held that "the principle of discovery gave European nations an

---

[30] "1823: Supreme Court rules American Indians do not own land." *National Library of Medicine*

absolute right to New World lands." This decision has been cited often since then to justify the negation of titles to land by Indigenous groups.

Not Just Bought and Sold

The system of slavery was not only a system of buying and selling human bodies. Enslaved people were treated as cattle, passed from generation to generation as livestock. As slave trade from Africa slowed down, it was also important for enslaved people to breed—again, very similar to how cattle are treated. If you thought enslavement, torture, and deprivation were horrific, there is yet another horrific practice to add to this ugly era of our shared history. Charles McGruder was not just a human being held captive by another human being. He was a breeder in agrarian forced-labor camps throughout the South. That means he was sent from labor camp to labor camp for the purpose of impregnating enslaved women to birth new enslaved people. That is some fucked-up shit. That is some shit to be reckoned with.

Indigenous Enslavers – Still Not White

This is a truly strange episode in our common history. In what became the Confederate States, the institution of slavery was encouraged among a group of Indigenous nations the US government was in the process of "civilizing." That is to say, enslaving Afrians and their descendants was encouraged among what historians have called the "Five Civilized Tribes," which include Cherokee, Chickasaw, Choctaw, Creek, and Seminole.

The 1619 Project, a book that grew out of a series of articles and a podcast from the *New York Times*, tells one story of a man named James Vann, the son of a Cherokee woman and Scottish man. Vann and his Cherokee children would become wealthy landowners, with farms that functioned as forced-labor camps in several southern states.

They would own human beings of African descent, as their white landowning counterparts did.

The trick? Participation as enslavers did not save them from having their land taken, not once but twice after being evicted by laws enacted first by southern state legislatures and then federally by President Andrew Jackson. That land grab culminated in the infamous Trail of Tears. In yet another strange twist, Indigenous enslavers, including the Vanns, were allowed to keep their human chattel as property, even as their lands were confiscated and given to white families.

Then, as the Civil War was set in motion, Indigenous enslavers had the mind-bending decision of whether to side with the Union, which they knew incapable of honoring a treaty, or the Confederacy, with which they shared the concept of slaveholding but who were no more trustworthy than their northern counterparts.

The legacy of the Doctrine of Discovery and invention of whiteness leads to exactly this kind of strange dichotomy in which a group can participate in African chattel slavery but also be considered subhuman.

Throughline: White Lies – "Everyone Participated in Transatlantic Slavery!" (so that makes it less bad for white people)

> I was on the phone recently when the white guy on the other end of the call said, "well, Africans participated in the slave trade too." To which I replied, "does that make it right?" The answer is NO!
>
> I have heard this argument many times before and it goes something like this: "Groups other than European traders, including Africans themselves, participated in the slave trade, so…" I think the argument is supposed to be that the Transatlantic slave trade was not unique in history and not only perpetrated by Europeans.
>
> While there is factual truth to the idea that Africans and others participated in the slave trade, it does not excuse the invention of a false racial hierarchy or an institution of slavery that dragged on for at least 400 years.
>
> Nice try, White Nonsense, but we see you!

That Time We Solved Racism: The Civil War and Reconstruction

This is the part of history that gets covered in civics classes all over the country. The question of enslaving humans came to a head. Compromise after compromise had been attempted and eventually slavery became simply incompatible with the plain language of the founding documents and the course of history.

Yay! The Civil War ended and slavery was abolished! White Nonsense solved! Even the most casual look at the historical record will show you this was definitely not the case.

Yes, we outlawed slavery in the United States.

Why did a bloody Civil War not solve the problem of White Nonsense? Why did the decades-long work of dismantling and outlawing chattel slavery not solve racism? People who had been held in bondage were now free to do as they pleased, right? Sure, there were some white people in the South who were a little bent out of shape about losing the war and losing their human property. But they were in some cases compensated for that.

Why did that not solve racism? Because the real problem was not solved—white people's nonsense still led them to believe they were superior to people of color. While African Americans were not technically the property of white people, the underlying supposition of white superiority was still in place.

And even as the Civil War was ending, wars in the still-forming western United States to secure white people's "manifest destiny" were resulting in the continued dehumanization and killing of Native Americans. The throughlines continued, even as the evil of chattel slavery was outlawed.

In order to end slavery as it existed up to that point, amendments to the Constitution needed to be written. The 13th Amendment abolished slavery "within the United States, or any place subject to their jurisdiction." The 14th Amendment granted full citizenship to all persons "born or naturalized in the United States."

The 13th Amendment was ratified in December of 1865 and the 14th Amendment in July of 1868. The amendments end slavery and offer full rights of citizenship and equal protection to all citizens under US law. This seems like remarkable progress.

This seemed like the end of White Nonsense.

But it wasn't. First of all, amendments don't automatically change hearts and minds. The deeply-ingrained fiction of racial superiority did not just die with the end of the war. But more importantly, the amendments left room for systemic racism to flourish in other ways.

To understand why this was the case, let's look at the language of the 13th and 14th Amendments to the Constitution.

The 13th Amendment reads:

Section 1
Neither slavery nor involuntary servitude, except as a punishment for crime whereof the party shall have been duly convicted, shall exist within the United States, or any place subject to their jurisdiction.

Section 2
Congress shall have power to enforce this article by appropriate legislation.

One phrase that has taken on a life of its own is "except as a punishment for crime whereof the party shall have been duly convicted." Over the coming century, White Nonsense would turn this into the prison industrial complex. According to [Federal Bureau of Prison](#)[31] statistics, as of 2022, Black males comprise 38% of the prison population, despite African Americans being 13% of the US population.

The Long Road to the 14th Amendment

The Constitution as it was written did not have much to say about citizenship. This may be a prime example of White Nonsense. In the minds of the framers, only white people could be considered citizens, so there wasn't really much to talk about.

But with the centuries-long question of chattel slavery finally answered, there needed to be a little more definition of what made a citizen of the United States.

There is perhaps no section of our Constitution more important in capturing the ideals of a United States elevated beyond

---

[31] "BOP Statistics: Inmate Race." *Federal Bureau of Prisons*, 22 October 2022

White Nonsense than the Equal Protection clause of 14th Amendment.

Section 1
All persons born or naturalized in the United States, and subject to the jurisdiction thereof, are citizens of the United States and of the State wherein they reside. No State shall make or enforce any law which shall abridge the privileges or immunities of citizens of the United States; nor shall any State deprive any person of life, liberty, or property, without due process of law; nor deny to any person within its jurisdiction the **equal protection** *of the laws.*

There is so much promise here. It seems to be setting the stage for true equality for citizens no matter where they come from or what level of melanin their skin contains. As we will see, a tiny clause in a constitutional amendment is no match for White Nonsense.

Okay, About That Equal Protection Clause...

The Equal Protection clause has always been problematic, in that history has shown that people of color, especially Black men, quantifiably do not enjoy equal protection under the law. Far from it. After the amendment was passed, lynchings that were attended as picnics throughout much of the US in the late 19th and early 20th centuries. More recently, "three strikes" laws of the 1990s meant longer prison sentences that disproportionately impacted Black people. Skating around Equal Protection brings us right into current events and the ongoing violence against Black bodies perpetrated by white people with or without a badge.

Put bluntly, the historic record is clear: we suck at equal protection. In a 7–1 decision in the 1896 *Plessy vs. Ferguson* decision, for example, the US Supreme Court established the idea of "separate but equal" accommodations. That did not go so well. And yes, the basis of that decision was overturned in *Brown v. Board of Education* 48 years later.

Yet people of color are still not afforded the same protections to this day, whether they are driving while Black or seeking asylum while Brown.

So back in the post-Civil-War era, we didn't solve racism because the underpinnings of white privilege and the presumptions of white superiority were still very much in place. Europeans had invested a lot of time, money, and intellect on the presumption that white people and European cultures were superior to other cultures.

If anything, after the Civil War there was a doubling down on rhetoric and pseudoscience that presumed or "proved" the superiority of people who called themselves "white."

White privilege was not going to just go softly into the night. The coming century would prove to be an ongoing reckoning between the stated ideals of our founding documents and the realities of power and privilege that white landowners fought to keep for themselves.

Reconstruction, Reparations, and a Return to the Status Quo

The period following the Civil War from 1865 through 1877 was a period known as Reconstruction. We've probably all heard that term, but what were the goals of Reconstruction? First, the restoration of the United States, so joining back the Union and secessionist states. Another goal–in hindsight eye-popping–was the transformation of southern society from an economy dependent on free labor to one that could accommodate free-market labor. (At the time, that meant treating workers horribly but giving them the freedom to experience horrible conditions wherever they wanted to go.) And finally, Reconstruction had the goal of enacting legislation that would enhance and provide greater equality under the law to previously-enslaved people.

A Brief History of White Nonsense

Historians such as David Blight and Heather Cox Richardson have made a strong case for why the US, following the Civil War, reverted back to the status quo of embracing White Nonsense so quickly, minus the technicality of chattel slavery. Slavery may have ended, but in its place was not a nation organized to make recompense for stolen years, stolen labor, or stolen potential for building wealth. White Nonsense—the ongoing presupposition that European Americans were superior—dictated that the recompense go not to the formerly enslaved but to the failed insurrectionists who fought to keep slavery in place.

> *"The Civil War and Reconstruction are the country's first great racial reckoning, and it brought about tremendous changes in law and in life—and then, of course, it brought about a counterrevolution that defeated much of it."* Historian David Blight, quoted in *Politico*.[32]

What does Blight mean by this? Reconstruction lasted around 12 years during which laws were passed protecting the rights of the formerly enslaved, African Americans were elected to fill congressional seats, and many other strides were taken to fulfill the ideal of forming a more perfect union. And then these gains were slowly, and sometimes quickly and violently, stripped away by systems from the Supreme Court to local community governments, and by active terrorists (often working in concert) in the South and North.

While the Union promised "40 acres and a Mule" to those held captive by other humans, nothing of the sort actually happened. Meanwhile, Confederates who lost "property" (aka fellow human beings) during the war were compensated. This is some for-real shit that happened. So instead of compensating the people who were treated as property and had their labor stolen for generations, the

---

[32] Stanton, Zack. "How Trumpism Is Becoming America's New "Lost Cause."" *Politico*, 21 January 2021

enslavers were compensated up to $300 per lost enslaved person. Thanks, Abe!

1875 Civil Rights Act

Toward the end of the Reconstruction Era, the US government actually passed civil rights legislation. The Civil Rights Act of 1875[33] guaranteed equal treatment in public accommodations and transportation and service on juries, among other provisions. The law made it illegal for anyone to facilitate the denial of these accommodations or services on the basis of color, race, or "previous condition of servitude."

It should make all of us wonder, it should be downright ponderous, to consider what might have happened had this original Civil Rights Act stood the test of time. As it actually happened, White Nonsense could not countenance this straightforward treatment (providing equal treatment!), especially of those in a "previous condition of servitude."

The Act was struck down by the US Supreme Court as unconstitutional in 1883, after which all semblance of Reconstruction was abandoned. They struck it down in an 8–1 decision with the reasoning that the Constitution does not extend to private businesses.

The decision, of course, paved the way for Jim Crow laws in the South and similar "stay away from white people" laws in the North. Oh, and if you got out of line, domestic terrorists would get up in your shit.

Dakota 38

Meanwhile, at the exact time the institution of chattel slavery was being abolished (with other forms of servitude and second-class

---

[33] US Senate. "Landmark Legislation: Civil Rights Act of 1875." *Senate.gov*

citizenship quickly put in its place), the Indigenous population was fighting for survival against the push for "manifest destiny" by European immigrants and their offspring.

One example of how this drama played out in what was becoming the western United States occurred on <u>December 26, 1862</u>.[34]

While the Union was fighting the Civil War against the secessionist states, they were also fighting wars against Native people. The US-Dakota War of 1862 is one of many that happened on what the US called "frontiers" but which the Indigenous population simply knew as home for the past hundreds and even thousands of years.

Since first contact with Europeans and the steady encroachment of the concept of "borders" into Turtle Island consciousness, the Dakota people had been confined to smaller and smaller portions of the land they once lived on. There were growing tensions and skirmishes between the Native folks and the white people who wanted to "settle" land the Dakota had settled into very nicely already.

In August, five European encroachers were killed in one such skirmish. The upshot of this event was that, several months later, the largest mass execution in US history took place.

The US-Dakota War occurred over 37 days. In the course of those events, U.S. Colonel Henry H. Sibley took 2,000 Dakota fighters and civilians into custody. After a sham trial, President Lincoln approved 39 executions, of which 38 were carried out. A huge scaffold was constructed, and the 38 were hanged one day after Christmas.

Indian Wars

What is more American than the image of the cowboy? What is more American than the rugged individual taking on the untamed

---

[34] Schilling, Vincent. "The Traumatic True History and Name List of the Dakota 38." *Indian Country Today*

wilderness until they reach the other side of the continent and take that shit over too? The problem, as ever: they didn't get there first.

Also as ever, the justification for this push westward (while other colonial powers had been pushing into what would become the American Southwest and Pacific Coast) was tinged with an unholy alliance between church and state. This is when the concept of "manifest destiny" came into vogue to explain the rush for land that other people already occupied. It was the white man's God-given right to do this.

Manifest destiny was happening in the US American West. This meant that though some human beings were technically gaining freedom, in the decades that followed, Indigenous people across the Great Plains, Southwest, and Pacific Northwest were being rounded up and killed or put into concentration camps on land no one else wanted.

This would be followed by decades of attempts to eradicate languages and cultures through education in "Indian Schools" which paradoxically were designed to take away "Indian" or Native-ness.

Of course, <u>battles over land</u> had been happening since Europeans set foot on American soil. And through the early 1800s, as English- and Spanish-speaking Europeans spread up from Central America and across from the 13 original English colonies, the original inhabitants took their stand.

So, after a war over the basic humanity of humans of African ancestry, the wars against Native people, with the stink of the Doctrine of Discovery, eugenics, etc. all over the endeavor, intensified in the waning decades of the 19th Century.

The 1864 Sand Creek Massacre is just one example of this, in which 148 peaceful Apache and Arapaho leaving winter camp were slaughtered by soldiers in what is now southeastern Colorado.

A Brief History of White Nonsense

The Battle of Little Bighorn (1876) and Wounded Knee (1890) are among the more famous battles in the waning days of the US government's land grab that was justified as manifest destiny.

L. Frank Baum, who would go on to write *The Wonderful Wizard of Oz*. In the *Saturday Pioneer*, the newspaper for Aberdeen, South Dakota, Baum wrote these chilling words following the massacre at Wounded Knee:

> *"The Pioneer has before declared that our only safety depends upon the total extermination of the Indians. Having wronged them for centuries we had better, in order to protect our civilization, follow it up by one more wrong and wipe these untamed and untamable creatures from the face of the earth."*[35]

Even recognizing the wrong done to the original inhabitants of the continent, White Nonsense saw them as a threat that needed to be eradicated. When that didn't come to pass, the next phase was to try eradicating language, culture, and traditions.

The Dawes Act

As access to land was increasingly denied to Indigenous people, and as an alternative to literally killing them all, Congress passed the General Allotment Act, also known as the Dawes Act, in 1887.

Provisions of the act included the head of each homesteading household receiving 160 acres of tribal land for farming or 360 acres for grazing. Single homesteaders would receive 80 acres. Title to the land would be held by the US government for 25 years. After 25 years, landholders would gain United States citizenship and fee simple title to the land.

---

[35] University of Warwick. *L Frank Baum's Editorials on the Sioux Nation*

A Brief History of White Nonsense

The upshot of this was that huge swaths of land were stolen from Indigenous people and opened up to homesteading by non-Native settlers. Ever wonder how "the West was won?" This is pretty much it.

It is estimated that Native Americans had access to 150 million acres on reservation lands alone before the Dawes Act. This was reduced to 38 million acres by the end of the Act in 1934.

Indian Schools

How did the Doctrine of Discovery and the fiction of white supremacy impact and continue to damage daily life for Native Americans in the late 19th and well into the 20th century?

Let's start with Richard Henry Pratt[36], who at 1879 the opening of the infamous Carlisle Indian Industrial School wrote that the best way to help Indigenous people was to "kill the Indian in him, and save the man." Pratt wrote about the equality of Native people with white people but believed that this equality would only be manifested by inculturation. Where generals and others before him wanted to stamp out Native populations, Pratt's goal was to stamp out Native cultures.

Well into the 20th century, that is the philosophy under which Indian Schools like Carlisle operated. Children sent to federal boarding schools for Native people were forbidden from speaking their own language. Their hair was cut. The attempt was to eradicate their culture. The attempt, in the madness of White Nonsense, was to "civilize" them. Families had to endure forced separation as children were removed from homes. Forced assimilation was put in place.

Ethnic cleansing had not worked, so cultural "cleansing" was the next alternative. So many languages died in this process. Many students died as well. A common feature of Indian Schools was a

---

[36] Bear, Charla. "American Indian Boarding Schools Haunt Many." *NPR*, 12 May 2008

graveyard. And when a child died from neglect and maltreatment, there was no family to mourn the loss. They were buried on site, and often these sites were made to disappear.

Biologist and author Robin Wall Kimmerer lives now in central New York, in part because she has a teaching position there. But as a Potowatami, her roots are in the Great Plains. In her excellent book, *Braiding Sweetgrass*[37], she recounts how her grandfather was taken from "Indian Territory" in Oklahoma to the Carlisle School in central Pennsylvania. After graduating, he felt he never fit in to either culture.

Two cities in which I have lived (I grew up in Phoenix and now live in Albuquerque) have roads named "Indian School" and ugly histories of stealing Native children from their homes and forcing them to live, and sometimes die, in residential schools.

Many Indian Schools were run by Christian denominations, and conversion to Christianity was an essential element of efforts at so-called civilizing.

Resistance during this era was common. When villages refused to send their children, reservation agents would withhold rations or forcibly remove children. While Robin Wall Kimmerer's grandfather was at Carlisle, his brother ran away and never returned to the school.

Throughline: Resistance – John Collier

In the resistance category, I have tried to focus on resistance to White Nonsense by Black and Indigenous people.

My exception to this rule is John Collier, a sociologist who, among other things, served as Commissioner of Indian Affairs in the Franklin Roosevelt administration from 1933-1945. Earlier in his career, he saw what was happening to Indigenous communities, especially after a 1921 visit to Taos Pueblo in New Mexico. This started him on a journey of advocacy focused on defending Indigenous

---

[37] Kimmerer, Robin Wall. *Braiding Sweetgrass*. Milkweed Editions, 2013

communities from forced assimilation, which put him at odds with the norm even among "progressive" white people of the time.

Resistance Today

Many communities are working at coming to terms with the legacy of Indian Schools and attempts to remove people from their language and culture and vice versa. When unmarked graves connected with the Indian School were recently discovered in Albuquerque, the city moved to memorialize the spot. It was here that a mass grave for Zuni, Apache, and Navajo children who went to the Albuquerque Indian Boarding School from 1882 to 1933 was found. In late 2021, Native leaders hosted a memorial for the children lost and ignored for decades.

Throughline: White Lies – "Our [White] Culture is the Definition of 'Civilized'"

> The movement to send Indigenous children to boarding schools is a perfect example of the lie of white culture as a "civilizing" influence. This started with de las Casas, was given voice by literary notables like Rudyard Kipling, and carries on today.
>
> Forced assimilation and attempts to erase culture are not "civilized." Far from it.
>
> When Black and Indigenous people and white allies talk about decentering whiteness, we are talking about the presumption of white norms and ways of doing things as THE norm. This covers everything from religious practices and parenting to business practices and hair texture and styles of dress. The pushback against those white-imposed norms is increasing, and the pressure to do away with them will hopefully not end until the nonsense ends.

Sundown Towns Up Top, Jim Crow on the Bottom

Northern liberals often enjoy feeling superior to their southern counterparts when it comes to the issue of race. We were on the side fighting slavery, and we didn't have Jim Crow! But the experience of people of color in the North was no picnic, from the sunset laws of the early to mid-1900s to the Chads and Karens of today calling police on Black people's suspicious behavior like walking, jogging, standing outside, and enjoying a cookout.

Sundown towns existed in every corner of the United States. The idea was that African Americans and other non-whites could pass through town or work in town, but after sunset, they should be gone or face the legal (or terrorist) consequences.

Laws of exclusion were the norm, from living in certain parts of a city to participating in organizations such as church, business, and other civic groups. How was this stuff legal?

Cruikshank Decision

In 1872, there was a fiercely disputed election for the position of governor in Louisiana. Unrest led to the Colfax Massacre[38], in which dozens of African Americans and three white people were killed in attempts to deprive African American citizens of the vote. It was a clear violation of the Enforcement Act of 1870 that prohibited "two or more people from conspiring to deprive anyone of their constitutional rights."

In a stunning reversal of Reconstruction policy, the First, Second, and Fourteenth Amendments, and the Enforcement Act itself, the Supreme Court held in the 1876 *United States v. Cruikshank* decision that the Bill of Rights did not apply to private citizens. In the case of the First Amendment right to assemble and Second Amendment right

---

[38] Lewis, Danny. "The 1873 Colfax Massacre Crippled the Reconstruction Era | Smart News." *Smithsonian Magazine*, 13 April 2016

to bear arms, the protections did not even extend to the actions of state governments. Holy crap! The result left African American citizens in very precarious positions when it came to voting rights and basically all other constitutional protections.

The upshot of the post-Reconstruction era, exemplified in the 1896 *Plessy v. Ferguson* decision, was to separate "equal" from "protection." The *Plessy* decision famously held that accommodations could be made separate but equal.

And while *Brown v. Board of Education* put an end to legal segregation over half a century later, Black People <u>can still experience anxiety</u> and fear traveling and just living their lives in the US. This fear is not imagined—it is well documented—and it did not arise out of thin air.

White Nonsense Baked in from the Beginning

By now you can see how the Doctrine of Discovery and the fiction of race were baked into the laws of the land, and how these laws and practices stretched well beyond a single era of our history.

Why did none of these remedies "solve racism"? Because as a nation, we do not yet have a common understanding of our history with White Nonsense at its core. We have not done the hard work of telling the truth to ourselves in order to truly form a more perfect union.

Chapter 4:
Throughlines: Progress and Regression

In the previous two chapters, we've seen how White Nonsense came into being in the first place and how those justifications for white-skin privilege were perpetuated throughout colonial days and the founding of the US, before and after the Civil War, and right up to today.

But we've made so much progress, right? What about Oprah? And those delightful Obamas? Those kids from the show *Reservation Dogs* are amazing. And, hey, White Nonsense resulted in some stolen land, but Native tribes have casinos now! Kevin Hart, Chris Rock, Beyoncé, and Jay-Z! We did it! We solved racism! Again!

Well, not exactly. I don't want to minimize progress because there is a lot to celebrate. We have come a long way from the overt assumption that European Americans are inherently superior to humans blessed with more melanin. That is good news. The bad news is that we do not yet have a collective sense of how that overtly racist history continues to shape us today.

A major throughline in the history of White Nonsense is how "progress" is measured. Hint: it's too often not measured by people of color. The point of this chapter is to show through history that the fiction of whiteness was often defended by force, and any progress toward true equality under the law and in everyday life has been hard-fought, halting, and thus far very incomplete.

True progress is made when whiteness is decentered. In other words, when white skin tones, hair textures, ways of speaking, dressing, etc. are regarded as not the default but as one expression among many.

Sweeties, we are not there yet. Throughout our shared history, there have been wonderful moments of progress and resistance along with regression back to White Nonsense. It's up to all of us to keep the momentum toward progress and resistance until the White Nonsense stops.

Progress: Juneteenth

June 19th, or Juneteenth, is celebrated as the date when the last state, Texas, finally recognized the outcome of the Civil War and declared all enslaved people free. In the city of Galveston, on this date in 1865, General Gordon Granger read *General Orders No. 3*, which stated: "The people of Texas are informed that, in accordance with a proclamation from the Executive of the United States, all slaves are free." This was two and a half years following the Emancipation Proclamation, and two months after General Lee surrendered at Appomattox.

Slavery was formally ended with the adoption of the 13th Amendment in December of that year.

Juneteenth has since become a celebration, a Black Independence Day that celebrates a fuller realization of the July 4th declaration that "all men are created equal."

In terms of the modern observance of Juneteenth as a federal holiday, it is Opal Lee who we have to thank. Born in 1926, her family moved from Marshall to Fort Worth, Texas when she was young. She spent much of her career as an educator in Fort Worth and later was a home school counselor. Following her retirement from education, she became an advocate for making Juneteenth a federal holiday, to the point where she is now known as the "grandmother of Juneteenth."

In her 90s, she was able to witness, on June 17, 2021, President Joe Biden signing legislation making Juneteenth a federal holiday.

Throughline: Resistance
Ida B. Wells

There are so many names and voices from the Civil War and post-Civil War era that are worth mentioning such as the biggies like Frederick Douglass and Harriet Tubman, of course. Books about those two from Scholastic Book sales are probably part of the reason I am writing this today. But there are so many others to know about.

I'd heard the name Ida B. Wells, but did not know much about her until researching for this book. The name is actually Ida B. Wells-Barnett. She was an African American investigative journalist and activist who documented lynchings and asked tough questions about what the government was NOT doing to protect citizens. So while nonsense like Cruikshank and Plessy were being decided in the Supreme Court, paving the way for a hands-off approach to political violence against African Americans, Wells-Barnett was not letting that be the end of the story.

She was disliked, of course, by those who supported or tolerated lynching. She was also disliked by many white suffrage activists who she called out for their silence on violence against African Americans. She was a founding member of the NAACP Women's Club, organized to address both civil rights and women's suffrage. From her birth in 1862 to her death in 1931, she was, in short, an anti-racist badass.

Regression: Wilmington Insurrection of 1898

While Ida B. Wells was fighting the good fight, Wilmington, North Carolina was just the sort of place she was fighting for. The Reconstruction era, brief as it was, provided some positive movement in terms of real political power for African Americans. Progress was happening in the post-Civil War South. One piece of evidence for this was the composition of elected officials in Wilmington, North Carolina. In the 1890s, Wilmington was the largest metropolitan area in North Carolina. But when Reconstruction was undone in the Supreme Court, statewide power started to shift to the Democrats—who at the time were the representatives of the former enslaving white planting class. Meanwhile, in Wilmington, which had a large African American population, Republicans remained in power.

Tensions were hot. On November 10th of 1898[39], spurred on by an editorial in the local paper that suggested widespread interracial sexual encounters between poor white women and African American men, the white citizenry was on edge.

That day, a former Confederate soldier, Alfred Moore Waddell, led a mob of angry white men to the editorial offices of the *Wilmington Daily Record*, where they looted the building and set it on fire.

Fourteen people of color lost their lives in the mob violence that resulted. Without any legal or military repercussions, Waddell and other leaders in the white mob took control of the Wilmington government.

The plain truth of what happened: a coup had succeeded against the duly-elected government of a United States city.

Regression: Home-Grown and State-Sponsored Terrorism

In the late 1800s, along with state-sponsored wars against Native populations from sea to shining sea, there were terrorists who often operated with the tacit consent of local government. In the post-Civil War time, as white people wondered what their place in the new

---

[39] LaFrance, Adrienne, and Vann R. Newkirk. "The Lost History of an American Coup D'État." *The Atlantic*, 12 August 2017

world order might be, groups like the Ku Klux Klan emerged to make sure the White-Nonsense-inspired order was maintained.

Strange Fruit

White people could not comprehend the full personhood of African Americans and Native Americans. It is difficult to erase hundreds of years of a worldview that puts white Europeans at the top of the social hierarchy. For centuries, white superiority had been baked into the way European Americans interacted with the first inhabitants of the North American continent and the people who they brought in as forced labor. When this balance of power has been threatened, terror ensues.

White terrorist organizations such as the Proud Boys and Oath Keepers, along with long-time white supremacist groups like the Ku Klux Klan, are coming out of the shadows. They are taking off their hoods and finding advocates in what used to be the fringes of the Republican party and, before a historic shift during the civil rights era of the 1950s and '60s, not even the fringes of the Democratic party.

Not Just a "Southern" Problem

Resistance to equality under the law was not just an issue in the former Confederacy. The KKK and other white terrorist organizations could and can still be found in every state in the Union.

This map of lynching between 1883 and 1941 shows that violent oppression of African Americans was not relegated to southern states. Not at all.

A Brief History of White Nonsense

Map created by and courtesy of David Rigby & Charles Seguin

Throughline: Resistance – Acknowledging Our Shared History

Three examples of understanding our history, decentering whiteness, and calling things by their name are three museums in very different parts of the country. America's Black Holocaust Museum is located in Milwaukee, Wisconsin. It is a place to explore the Black experience in the United States from before captivity to the present.

The Legacy Museum in Montgomery, Alabama explores the connection between enslavement and mass incarceration. It features a memorial the museum describes as "dedicated to the legacy of enslaved Black people, people terrorized by lynching, African Americans humiliated by racial segregation and Jim Crow, and people of color burdened with contemporary presumptions of guilt and police violence."

The Indian Pueblo Cultural Center is located in Albuquerque, New Mexico and explores the unique and ever-evolving cultures of the 19 Pueblo Indigenous communities. It includes museum and gallery space, along with a kitchen and restaurant featuring Native cuisine.

There are probably museums and cultural centers near you where the fullness of the US American experience is explored. I encourage you to seek those places out.

Regression: 1921 Tulsa Race Massacre

The abiding myth of white superiority could not handle the rise of African Americans to positions of wealth and privilege. Nowhere is this seen more clearly in the early decades of the 20th century than in the Tulsa Race Massacre. This story is getting more attention in recent years, but I certainly had heard nothing about it in my formal education or through a large chunk of my adult life. If you are a white reader, I imagine your experience is similar.

So what the hell happened? In segregated Tulsa, Oklahoma, a neighborhood called Greenwood was home to a prosperous Black population. Businesses were booming in Greenwood. The whole of Tulsa was doing well, so it would seem like there would at least be a "live and let live" attitude that allowed a rising tide to lift all boats.

But Greenwood was getting a reputation. It was becoming known as "Black Wall Street" for its healthy business climate and the growing wealth of Black business owners and professionals in the neighborhood.

Then the story takes a repulsively familiar turn. A young Black man is accused of…it's not quite clear…with a white woman. <u>An account on History.com</u> tells of a young Black man, Dick Rowland, entering an elevator in an office building. A young, white woman named Sarah Page was the elevator operator. At some point, Page screamed and Rowland quickly left. The next morning, he was arrested.

While in police custody, a small group of Black men went to guard Rowland against lynching, and a huge crowd of white Tulsans overpowered them. This set of circumstances led to the looting and burning of the Greenwood neighborhood by mobs of white Tulsans, some of whom were deputized by Tulsa police.

Progress: The Concept of Race Gets its Comeuppance with Franz Boas

The idea that race is a social construct and not a biological fact comes from the pioneering work of German-born anthropologist Franz Boas[40], born in 1858.

His concepts of Cultural Relativism were radical for the time. All education is relative, all culture is relative. According to Boas, concepts like "primitive" and "advanced" are not theories that hold up.

For 500 years, the fiction of race and the racial hierarchy that put Caucasians at the top had gone largely unchallenged (at least by so-called Caucasians). The man who became known as "the father of modern anthropology" put a big dent in that, at least in academic circles.

He moved to the United States in 1886. Ten years later, he began teaching at Columbia University and became their first professor of anthropology. In 1911 he delivered a series of lectures debunking the idea of Western superiority. His books were burned by the Nazis in the 1930s, and his PhD from Kiel University in Germany was revoked.

Boas challenged the conventions of white European ideas that some "races" are superior and some are suited to servitude.

Even progressive thought at that time often meant being devoted to raising up "backwards" people. This is precisely why, as US troops battled against Nazi ideas of "a master race," life in the US was based on similar thinking.

Zora Neale Hurston, Margaret Mead, and others were drawn to the work of Boas.

Detractors, from the late Allan Bloom to the current Amy Wax, have decried these efforts to chip away at centuries of racist

---

[40] Biography. "Franz Boas -." *Biography*, 2 April 2014

presuppositions embedded in the Doctrine of Discovery and the fictional idea of melanin-based race that was presented as fact. But the unambiguous facts of history and how they tie to current events create a clear picture of the reality of White Nonsense.

Throughline: Resistance – The Great Migration

In response to the failure of the US government to protect African American citizens from white terrorist threats and actions, around six million African Americans fled the Jim Crow South. Seeking political asylum within their own country, this exodus began in the early 1900s and some historians say it lasted until around 1970.

Again, I don't want this to be a book that puts a lot of onus on the South and lets the North slide. The Great Migration happened when the North experienced a labor shortage. The supply of cheap labor from places like Ireland and eastern Europe was drying up, so African Americans from the South could fill in that gap. The hope was that the move from sharecropping—which was basically wage and debt slavery—would mean African American families could finally fully participate in the benefits of citizenry. Things were better in the North, but "better" is a relative term. Black men found work in factories and slaughterhouses or as porters on train lines, most famously the Pullman line. Black women, unsurprisingly, had fewer options, most often finding work cleaning the homes of white people.

Whatever the limitations Black families faced as they moved North, I also don't want to make light of how big a shift in self-determination this was. The Harlem Renaissance, Motown, and the jazz of Louis Armstrong, Miles Davis, and John Coltrane—all of this can be traced to the Great Migration. We probably would not have the works of Toni Morrison or Langston Hughes without the Great Migration. We might not have the work of Prince or the rivalry between East Coast and West Coast hip hop without the Great Migration.

There were three main paths from the Deep South to all points north. Along the East Coast, migration tended toward Washington DC, Baltimore, and Philadelphia up through Boston. While opportunities were more abundant, those cities are not exactly known for their racial equity and harmony, even today.

From Mississippi, one might head north up to Cleveland, Chicago, or Detroit. Again, there is so much rich culture developed over the last century in those places. Yet racism was certainly not solved. Chicago is known as one of the most segregated cities in the country. And let's not forget about Detroit. Motown would not exist without the Great Migration. Plentiful factory jobs were to be had in Motor City. Then white flight in the '60s and '70s led to a deeply segregated population between the city and its suburbs.

From Louisiana, the road might take a sharecropper family to Texas, on to California, and even Seattle. Doors opened in the entertainment industry, but White Nonsense persisted in the kinds of entertainment that were considered "all American." And while the tech industry is flourishing in the Bay Area and Seattle, it remains a predominantly white and male industry.

Regression: Housing Discrimination

The next three sections on housing, education, and incarceration are where we see the clearest evidence of the systemic nature of racism and how long-ago ideas like the Doctrine of Discovery and the fiction of white supremacy reverberate into today.

Redlining and Implications for Today

To look for evidence of the throughlines of racism as it connects directly today with generational wealth, look no further than <u>housing discrimination</u>.

A Brief History of White Nonsense

Non-whites have historically had much less access to this avenue for building wealth. During the 1940s and 50's as white families were building a massive new middle class, Black families and other people of color were not even able to apply for a mortgage, they were barred from certain neighborhoods and whole towns. Lending was not available to them. How could that be?

Access to mortgage lending was pivotal in the rise of the white middle class. The ability to purchase real estate and build equity in a home meant that equity was available to build wealth and make a better life from generation to generation. After World War II, one of the key components of the G.I. Bill provided access to low-interest mortgage loans. Yet Jim Crow laws in the South and 100% legal racial covenants in property deeds in the North—that is, laws that overtly excluded Blacks, Jews, and other ethnic and religious minorities—kept Black veterans and others from purchasing property. These restrictions were upheld by the US Supreme Court before the rise of the white middle class in a 1926 ruling, and did not officially end until the Fair Housing Act of 1968. Many such covenants are still on the books.

The upshot was that Black soldiers who had risked their lives fighting for their country were left out of the main source of wealth-building afforded by the G.I. Bill.

But we're past that, right? We have the Fair Housing Act, so we solved racism—again!

On paper, things have gotten a LOT better in terms of equity in access to housing for all ethnic groups. In my lifetime (I was born in 1967), the Fair Housing Act of 1968 was put into place. So for most of US History up until Generation X, access to housing was overtly unfair, overtly advantaging people who thought of themselves as white.

The Fair Housing Act prohibits discrimination concerning the sale, rental, and financing of housing based on race, religion, national origin, sex, (and as amended) handicap and family status.

Discrimination became illegal, so why does housing discrimination persist? Study after study shows that redlining persists in lending. In whatever part of the country you may be trying to secure a mortgage, if you are a person of color, your chances of being denied are significantly higher than for white applicants. <u>One recent study</u>[41] found this to be the case in 48 US cities where research was conducted.

How Zoning Laws Continue to Exclude

When systemic access to wealth is denied to you, you tend to be on the lower end of the economic spectrum. So while zoning laws don't get as specific as saying "people of color are not welcome here," the effect is the same.

The US Supreme Court banned the use of <u>zoning laws</u> that explicitly used race as a criteria in the 1917 decision *Buchanan v. Warley*. This did not deter city and regional planners, who found more creative ways of segregating ethnic groups.

For instance, zoning laws specifying that certain areas can only have single-family dwellings have been used to keep lower-income people away from higher-income and middle-class neighborhoods. The cascading effects on overall health outcomes and the wealth gap between white families and families of color are not surprising.

One area where housing discrimination hits the fan the hardest is in public education.

Progress or Regression? Public Education

Things are not great these days in public education. As I write, there is a concerted effort around the country, especially in suburban school districts, to roll back whatever little progress has been made

---

[41] Glantz, Aaron, and Emmanuel Martinez. "Modern-day redlining: Banks discriminate in lending." *Reveal | from The Center for Investigative Reporting*, 15 February 2018

regarding diversity, equity, and inclusion around race and other factors. There is resistance from the dominant white culture to both a full and accurate telling of our shared history and to creating a more inclusive learning environment.

After the civil rights era, White Nonsense had to be a bit more nuanced, at least before 2016. Nice white people were just trying to live their lives. But in order to live in neighborhoods where White Nonsense could be the norm, laws needed to be enacted.

In areas where poverty is concentrated, there are manifold problems with funding for education high on the list. Without access to property taxes from high-value homes and businesses, school districts in lower-income areas struggle to create a positive learning environment.

Again, none of this is happening by accident. Having policies to teach the truth of history in age-appropriate ways and creating curriculum and a learning environment that decenter whiteness is great. But until funding of education is decoupled from property taxes and housing discrimination is eliminated, there will be inevitable inequities in the way children are educated.

Resegregation After *Brown vs. Board*

When the Supreme Court undid the 1896 "separate but equal" framework developed in *Plessy v. Ferguson*, it was the culmination of decades of work by organizations like the NAACP.

But in a world where whiteness is defined as the "norm," whiteness will find a work-around to stay separated. And in the intervening years since *Brown v. Board*, Black, Indigenous, and people of color parents have expressed a great deal of skepticism about having their children educated in a system centered in whiteness.

Which is really where we are today. Today in the school district where my children were educated, a new board member publicly raised concerns about a curriculum that is not sufficiently "Western-centric."

School board meetings across the country are battle grounds for concerns about teaching actual history as well as Diversity, Equity, and Inclusion initiatives. White parents are saying the quiet part out loud. They do not want their children to become uncomfortable about our common history.

Well, guess what? I had to sit through calculus and chemistry. That made me very uncomfortable! It's called learning.

Between the *Brown v. Board* decision in 1955 and now, a lot happened. Many communities fought desegregation for decades after the Supreme Court decision. Conservative white Christians started the private school movement. White flight from urban centers to new suburbias happened, aided by housing and mortgage discrimination and those conveniently racist zoning laws.

White Nonsense found a way to resegregate public schools, and most public education remained centered in whiteness as the norm.

Regression: Mass Incarceration

Remember that clause in the 13th Amendment? *"Neither slavery nor involuntary servitude,* **except as a punishment for crime** *whereof the party shall have been duly convicted, shall exist within the United States…"*

With that phrase, "except as a punishment for crime," White Nonsense found a massive loophole to the whole slavery thing. It is no mystery why the incarceration of people of color and especially African American men is so out of whack as a percentage of the population. As noted previously, the prison population for Black men is way out of whack compared with their overall percentage in the US population. This is no accident.

Here is just one example. Harvard Law School's Criminal Justice Policy program looked at the raw data in Massachusetts from a 2016 report and found that incarcerated African Americans "received more severe charges, harsher sentences and less favorable outcomes than their white counterparts."

What accounts for this? We have heard this story before, and it is true not just in Massachusetts. Here are some details about what that [study from Harvard University](#) found about systemic racism in the Massachusetts criminal justice system: A greater likelihood for police to stop Black drivers and investigate Black residents. Black suspects were charged with breaking laws that carried worse penalties than white suspects. Black suspects were less likely to be offered plea bargains. When found guilty, sentences were longer, while the average white felon has committed a more severe crime than the average Black prisoner.

Study after study shows similar data pointing unmistakably to systemic racism in the criminal justice system. What might an anti-racist judicial system look like? Maybe like Los Angeles District Attorney George Gascón, elected in 2020. He ran on a platform of criminal justice reform, and went on to enact reforms as promised. Under his leadership the Los Angeles DAs office does not charge juveniles as adults. They did away with cash bail for nonviolent offenses. Charges related to misdemeanor substance abuse and mental illness were no longer handled by the LA justice system. Which led to a [petition to remove him from office](#).

Ava DuVernay's film *13th* does an excellent job of building the throughlines from slavery to convict "leasing" to the war on drugs, all leading to high incarceration rates for Black and Brown people.

Analyzing Regression: Why This Shit Keeps Happening

In high school, I got to fly from my home in Phoenix to Washington, D.C. for a week's intensive study of the US government in a program called Close Up. I have many fond memories of that time, including picking up copies of books by Locke, Hume, and other Enlightenment thinkers.

One memory that for years I didn't know what to do with: I wound up sharing a hotel room with some guys from Atlanta or somewhere like that. Nice young white men. They had a Confederate flag that they hung up in the room. In 1985, as a 16-year-old from the Southwest, I was curious but didn't think much of it. Then one of the teachers who was a chaperone on the trip and an African American came into the room. He told them to take that symbol of hate down immediately. I remember the fairly thoughtful discussion that took place, with my Atlanta friends talking about the "new South" and the teacher basically saying as kindly as possible: "Um, there is nothing new about racist oppression, but thanks for playing."

We need to understand these symbols. We need to understand the legacy of White Nonsense; we need to confront it so things can change at a deeper level. While these residual ideas of racial superiority still linger, we need to answer for them.

I hear the counterargument. All. The. Time. What good does it do to remind white people of the bad decisions made on their behalf in the past? Who the hell cares? We are all well aware that the land we live on was stolen several generations ago and that many of the Europeans who stole it also paid for ownership rights to other human beings several generations ago.

What's that got to do with me? I didn't do those things. It's terrible, but it's tucked away in the past. We need to get over it and move on.

That sounds appealing, especially to the descendants of those naughty Europeans. But the words of Southern Gothic author William Faulkner are instructive here: "The past is never dead. It's not even past."[42]

---

[42] Faulkner's 1951 play, *Requiem for a Nun* is the source for this, one of his most famous lines of prose.

A Brief History of White Nonsense

The problem is that the white supremacist underpinnings of the Doctrine of Discovery and the concept of race were not questioned for most of the intervening years between 1493 and now. What? That's not true, is it?

Well, my argument here is that US history mostly shows a VERY slow and begrudging walk from white European "exceptionalism" toward equality and such basic principles as people of color simply "mattering." The Doctrine of Discovery and the invention of a racial hierarchy were the key enabling factors that slow progress, that keep us from sprinting toward a better now and future. Even if people weren't being sold into slavery or their land violently taken from them, the fiction of European superiority remained. It remains in violent actions against Black, Indigenous, and other people just trying to live their lives in peace, freedom, and equality. It remains in assumptions that center whiteness as the de facto norm in society. It remains in patronizing actions that presume it is the burden of white people to lift up others who are "less fortunate." Through all these means, the structures that make up our society have been slow-walking a march toward true equality.

That's not just me thinking out loud. This book is an examination of US history that clearly and unmistakably shows this slow-walk, informed directly by the Doctrine of Discovery and the fiction of race.

White people maybe felt bad about slavery. That stuff was super mean. And maybe they felt bad about the stolen land taken from people who already lived here. But that's just how things were back then. That has nothing to do with today.

Yet there remains in society both outwardly hostile racism—the KKK kind of racism—and the Rudyard Kipling "white man's burden" kind of racism. Both keep showing up and will be the norm until we completely remove these centuries-long assumptions about white superiority from our thinking and the institutions those thoughts create.

Economic Consequences

It is not difficult to see how all of this deep structural-level nonsense has led to a wealth gap. White people have had vastly more opportunities over the past centuries, especially the last one, to build generational wealth. The centuries-long assumptions about the place of white people in the social order has made this result inevitable.

The data is abundant. African Americans and Native Americans have been excluded from these opportunities and still are passed over for mortgages and other lending instruments that build wealth over time.

For instance, white Chicagoans viewed the Great Migration as calamitous as the Great Fire. When humans are equated with calamity, their personhood is called into question. This reverberates through history.

Just Get Over It

Why can't we/they just get over it? Why can't we all just get along? The throughlines of the Doctrine of Discovery, the invention of race as a social construct, pseudoscience that invents ways to put European people and culture at the top of any list they are making—none of this has been fully dismantled, and it has led to systems of advantage and outright oppression that continue to this day.

Chapter 5:
The Hard Work of Dismantling Systems

As I began this project, I understood the systemic nature of racism, sort of. I understood our basic history and that white privilege continues to exist in every facet of US society.

It was the "why" that was bothering me, that led me to keep digging, keep asking questions. Why are the throughlines of history not taught more explicitly so we can better understand our present circumstances? Why don't new laws and public policies end racial discrimination that perpetuates the lie of white supremacy?

Of course, it is much, much easier (for white people) not to examine the history of White Nonsense. It is much, much easier to focus on progress and write lists of very successful people of color. How can racism exist if Oprah is a billionaire, right?

We all have lives to live, and in many ways we are all—regardless of our ethnic backgrounds—just trying to live life, get by, and thrive as best we can. That's what most of us want, and there are plenty of inspiring stories of people of different ethnic backgrounds overcoming prejudice and just being human beings together.

But the pernicious nature of White Nonsense—of that original lie that white lives matter more—does not let up. The institutions that were built to keep on top the people who think of themselves as white do not change quickly or easily. Regardless of the intentions of individual police officers, judges, teachers, medical professionals, or tech bros, systemic racism persists as history and current events clearly demonstrate.

A Brief History of White Nonsense

What Does "Dismantling Systems" Mean?

This book is meant to provide a clear picture of how systemic, institutional racism came to be. It started with the many justifications for colonization, the ongoing justifications for slavery, and attempts at genocide and marginalization of Native Americans. The systems and institutions were put in place for the benefit of people of the right kind of European descent and to the detriment of people who are, in point of fact, collectively members of the global majority. That in itself may be a clue as to why the people who benefit from whiteness are fighting so hard to keep these systems in place.

Because these systems are so entrenched from before the founding of this country, anti-racist legal remedies are ALWAYS met with resistance by the white power structure. The structures of racism are pernicious as the historic evidence and current events bear out. Historically and right into the present, there has not been the political will to fully recognize and dismantle the systems and institutions that have been put in place to keep the bulk of privilege in the hands of people who think of themselves as white.

Here is a definition of institutional racism from the book *Teaching for Diversity and Social Justice*[43]: "The network of institutional structures, policies, and practices that create advantages and benefits for Whites, and discrimination, oppression, and disadvantage for people from targeted racial groups. The advantages created for Whites are often invisible to them. Or are considered 'rights' available to everyone as opposed to 'privileges' awarded to only some individuals and groups."

In my anti-racism training with Crossroads and then Damascus Road in the early 2000s, we did an exercise called "Better/Worse" in which we, as a group of people from all kinds of ethnic and economic

---

[43] Adams, Maurianne, et al., editors. *Teaching for Diversity and Social Justice*. Routledge, 2022, p 93

backgrounds, thought through how things have gotten better in terms of dismantling racism and how they have gotten worse.

I'd encourage you to take a mental inventory of what you think is better and worse about the current state of White Nonsense in US America. Whatever is on your list in the "better" column, it is clear that much work remains. With that in mind, let's look at a few ways we can actively move toward a better, more equitable future.

Politics and Resistance

Resistance to and action against the lie of white supremacy is inherently political. The status quo demands that systems in the United States implicitly or explicitly center and benefit whiteness. Yet resistance has been happening from the beginning. What can resistance look like today in an era of "anti-wokeness" and what many refer to as a whitelash against demographic changes and progress toward an anti-racist society? Here are a few examples.

Decolonization

You may have come across calls to "decolonize" various aspects of society. Decolonization is basically a call to decenter whiteness as the primary frame of reference for what is "right" or "normal."

This might come in the form of individuals reclaiming language, dress, foods, and folkways all the way to larger stands taken by communities to reclaim stolen land, personhood, and culture. For instance, maybe you have heard about the CROWN Act, which is an effort by the Coalition to Advance Anti-Hair Discrimination Legislation to end discrimination—especially in the workplace—against natural Black hair. For many decades and in too many places, the wide varieties of Black hair that does not meet white expectations of straight or slightly curly has been seen as "unprofessional." That is, of course, nonsense.

Decolonization efforts can be seen in Indigenous communities who are literally reclaiming land stolen from them and accessing sacred lands they have been barred from accessing. Bears Ears is an example of these kinds of efforts. Recently, an inter-tribal coalition of the Hopi Tribe, Navajo Nation, Ute Mountain Tribe, Pueblo of Zuni, and Ute Indian Tribe have formed the <u>Bears Ears Inter-Tribal Coalition</u>. This is an effort to protect the Bears Ears cultural landscape in the area of what is now the four corners where Arizona, Utah, Colorado, and New Mexico meet.

I recently joined an effort by faith communities in the US and Canada to undo the harms of colonialism. It's called the <u>Dismantling the Doctrine of Discovery Coalition</u>. We have big goals to join with Indigenous-led efforts similar to Bears Ears. Along with that, we have a set of actions local faith communities can take to recognize the land where their buildings stand and whether where members live is unceded territory of Indigenous communities. Who lived there first? Are they still in the neighborhood? (I live in Albuquerque on the unceded lands of the Sandia and Isleta people. They are very much still here.)

Voting Rights

Voting rights is another throughline that brings White Nonsense from the founding of the nation into the present. Of course, in the beginning it was only white landowning men who had the right to vote. The vote expanded over the years until, low and behold, men in the global majority and eventually even women of every ethnicity could, technically, vote.

Of course, White Nonsense did not love the idea of what is called universal suffrage—the right of all adult citizens to vote.

A Brief History of White Nonsense

Take the Voting Rights Act of 1965 as an example. Just two years before I was born, this federal law criminalized literacy and other tests or "devices" states and municipalities were using to suppress the votes of people of color.

We solved racism, again! Nope, the Voting Rights Act was challenged in court but mostly upheld—until 2013.

That's when the Supreme Court voted in *Shelby County v. Holder* to strike down the section of the Voting Rights Act called the "coverage formula" in Section 4(b). Jurisdictions with a history of racially-discriminatory rules were the subject of this section. The coverage formula held, in part, that a "test or device" such as a literacy test, could not be used to deny voting rights to otherwise qualified people.

In 2021, Republican state legislatures around the country worked and often succeeded in enacting voter suppression laws with the claim that voter fraud was a serious problem that needed to be addressed. Loyola Law professor Justin Levitt conducted a project looking at national voting data from 2000 to 2014. He identified only 31 cases of voter fraud (impersonation) out of more than one billion ballots cast.[44]

Oregon is one of a number of states that have held elections primarily by mail, even before the COVID-19 pandemic. Since the year 2000, the state has sent out over 100 million mail ballots. There have been fewer than 15 cases of proven voter fraud during that time.

Yet conservative groups like the Heritage Foundation have a database of voter fraud and seem to consider it a big problem. Who is telling the truth? The Heritage Foundation found 143 convictions related to voter fraud in municipal, state, and federal elections, which represents dramatically less than 1% of votes cast.

---

[44] Levitt, Justin. "A comprehensive investigation of voter impersonation finds 31 credible incidents out of one billion ballots cast." *The Washington Post*, 6 August 2014

Another example is the 2021 sham audit by friends of the 45th president of the US. They too found no significant fraud that would have changed the outcome of the election in Maricopa County, AZ, much less the United States. So, when news sources repeat ad nauseum that there is no widespread voter fraud, it is clear that they are telling the truth.

Why is one party bent on suppressing the vote? And let me be clear, if it served the interests of the Democratic Party, I have no doubt that similar actions would be taken in Democratic-controlled legislatures. White Nonsense finds the most ideal conditions in which to grow. Until around the 1950s, that was the Democratic Party. Since then, the tables have turned, and in recent years the Republican Party has gone well beyond coded language and more brazenly embraced white supremacist ideas. Voter suppression is just one example of this.

The Problem with Mattering

All that has happened between the late 1400s and today brings us to yet another moment of reckoning. In response to police killings of unarmed Black men, movements like Black Lives Matter (BLM) have emerged. The blowback to these movements in the form of opposition in schools to anything about racism in our history shows how BLM is a direct assault on White Nonsense.

The purveyors of White Nonsense and those who do not understand the throughlines of history are not amused by BLM. As comedian and SNL head writer Michael Che says in one of his stand-up routines, "It's a pretty low bar. We just want to matter. And people still have a problem with that."

I just heard a radio host and caller anxiously speaking about what they believe is "Critical Race Theory" taught in public elementary and high schools these days. "They don't call it that, of course," the caller said. "They call it teaching about social justice." The host agreed and gave the caller plenty of opportunity to continue to opine.

A Brief History of White Nonsense

In school districts like Pennridge in suburban Pennsylvania (where my children graduated as this nonsense was starting to rise), board members openly speak anxiously about making sure enough "Western voices" are heard in the curriculum. They're not even bothering to speak in code these days. And we are a nation that is now expected to be opposed to justice. At least if we were living in a sitcom, the caller would say, "Oh, I hear it now. That's ridiculous."

Movements like BLM and Diversity, Equity, and Inclusion (DEI) initiatives in schools are a threat to the white status quo. In this world created out of White Nonsense, voices of people of color have always been seen as a threat, and Black bodies in particular have always been under threat. In the digital age, this threat is well-documented. Comedians and meme-creators joke about the Chads and Karens of the world feeling threatened by Black bodies walking their pets, enjoying a cookout, waiting outside an apartment for friends, etc. but the threat is no joke.

Black Lives Matter is the current iteration, as I write, of the struggle for the equal protection of black bodies under the law. Because as we have seen over and over in the history of White Nonsense, laws can be written that seem to provide equal protection. But White Nonsense always seems to find a work-around.

The perpetrators of clear and obvious violence against Black bodies keep finding protection that is "more equal" than those of the Black bodies they destroy—for driving, walking, shopping, selling cigarettes, sleeping at home, etc. ad nauseum—whatever these Black bodies are doing, violence against them rarely ends in consequences that fit the crime. Most often, it is found that no crime has been committed against these now inert Black bodies.

These are the current events I am living through. I am white, so living through these events is a given.

When I see BLM ridiculed, I see it as one more example of the fear implicit in a world that is experiencing rapid demographic change.

A Brief History of White Nonsense

I write this at the end of Donald Trump's years in the White House, and I fervently hope I don't have to come back and rewrite this section when he gets a second, nonconcurrent term.

Much has been written about the Trump years already. My observation is that the fervent loyalty of his base is symptomatic of the unfinished business that is White Nonsense.

White Fears, White Reckoning

As I write this, the underpinnings of White Nonsense are being questioned by some and violently defended by others in ways we haven't seen since the civil rights movement of the 1950s and '60s.

Groups like the Heritage Foundation and Hillsdale College make opposition to what they incorrectly define as Critical Race Theory a major aspect of their work and identity. Because the truth is that white Europeans are a global minority and quickly becoming a minority in the United States. Examining our common history and current events is VERY uncomfortable because the facts are unambiguous: Europeans invented whiteness and made it the "norm."

The sham is being outed, so the work of whitewashing history—pretending these things are in the past—is a full-time job for those who want to maintain the status quo. Books like this are "sewing racial division." Writing about this means the author "hates white people."

Nope. Wrong again, White Nonsense. The reckoning is necessary, but the entrenched, centuries-old systems that have propped up the myth of white supremacy are not going quietly into the night.

Where We Go From Here

On the anniversary of the January 6th attack, members of the cast of the musical *Hamilton* sang the song "Dear Theodosia." On the birth of his daughter Theodosia, as the colonies consider revolution against England, Aaron Burr, promises to lay a strong foundation, to "bleed and fight for you. We'll make it right for you."

Introducing the song during a session of Congress, *Hamilton* creator Lin-Manuel Miranda said[45], "We are all stewards of the American experiment, working to pass down to our children and our grandchildren a more perfect union that treats all its citizens with fairness and equity. We should never take our rights and liberty for granted and we must remain committed to finding a way forward together."

A multi-ethnic cast singing this song provides a clear message: we have much to do and undo to get to that perfect Union. I tear up every damn time I hear this song, especially in the context of saying an emphatic "NO!" to the White Nonsense embedded in the January 6th insurrection. From the Founders right to each of us today, we know another world is possible. But we've got to fight for it, and part of that fight is simply telling the truth.

This book is meant to be a clear presentation of the historical record. There are many, even currently, who are trying to whitewash history.

Confronting and reckoning with a historic evil that is still being perpetrated is challenging to say the least. But the historic record shows without ambiguity: the role of White Nonsense, the fiction of whiteness, and the facts of white-skin privilege are unambiguous. There are not multiple ways look at this history, unless you are unabashed in your belief in white supremacy. How we go about equity

---

[45] "Lin-Manuel Miranda, 'Hamilton' cast members help commemorate Jan. 6 attack." *The Hill*, 6 January 2022

and equality—how we create the circumstances where equal treatment under the law is a fact and not a hope—*that* is where there is room for discussion and debate. How do we move forward beyond White Nonsense?

The politics of moving forward and reckoning with a 500-plus-year-old enduring stain is challenging. As I look at the history of the past 30 years especially, I see a lot of white fear about this reckoning. White people need to move beyond that, join in the process of decentering whiteness, and rebuild more just systems that are meant to work for everyone.

RESOURCES

Like the book itself, this list is far from exhaustive. But if you are looking for a deeper dive into the issues presented, this is a good start.

Books That Shaped My Formation as an Anti-Racist:
Maya Angelou, *I Know Why the Caged Bird Sings*, 1969, Random House.
Powerfully and beautifully written autobiography. A book that should be read for so many reasons.

Dee Brown, *Bury My Heart at Wounded Knee*, 1970, Holt, Rinehart & Winston.
I remember paging through this book from my brother's bookshelf as a kid.

Ralph Ellison, *Invisible Man*, 1952, Random House.
I read this book in college and was drawn in by the narrative and the exploration of personal experience with systemic racism in North and South.

Shelby Steele, *The Content of Our Character*, 1998, Harper Perennial.
I include this book not because I agree with many of its ideas, but because it forced me to think more clearly about systemic racism.

Books We Should All Be Reading:
Sarah Augustine, *The Land is Not Empty*, 2021, APG
Mark Charles and Soong-Chan Rah, *Unsettling Truths*, 2019, InterVarsity Press
Roxanne Dunbar-Ortiz, *An Indigenous People's History of the United States*, 2015, Beacon Press
John Graham, *Plantation Theory*, 2021, Mynd Matters Publishing

A Brief History of White Nonsense

Nikole Hannah-Jones, et al., *The 1619 Project*, 2021, New York Times Company
Sharon Hurley-Hall, *I'm Tired of Racism*, 2022, Lime Tree Media
Ibram X. Kendi, *How to Be an Anti-Racist*, 2019, One World
Elizabeth Leiba, *I'm Not Yelling*, 2023, Mango
Ijeoma Oluo, *So You Want to Talk About Race*, 2019, Seal Press
Nell Irvin Painter, *The History of White People*, 2011, W. W. Norton and Co.
Heather Cox Richardson, *How the South Won the Civil War*, 2022, Oxford University Press

Documentaries:

13th, Directed by Ava Duvernay, 2016
Synopsis: An exploration of the intersection of race, justice, and the criminal justice system, with the 13th amendment as both justification and roadmap.

Dawnland, Directed by Adam Mazo and Ben Pender-Cudlip, 2018.
Synopsis: For decades, child welfare authorities have been removing Native American children from their homes to "save them from being Indian." In Maine, the first official Truth and Reconciliation Commission in the United States begins a historic investigation. Dawnland goes behind-the-scenes as this historic body grapples with difficult truths, redefines reconciliation, and charts a new course for state and tribal relations.

I am Not Your Negro, Directed by Raoul Peck, 2017
Synopsis: A work based on the unfinished manuscript, "Remember This House" by James Baldwin, a reflection on the lives and assassinations of his friends, Medgar Evers, Malcolm X and Martin Luther King, Jr..

www.ingramcontent.com/pod-product-compliance
Lightning Source LLC
Chambersburg PA
CBHW051347040426
42453CB00007B/448